Spiritual Fragrances

ONLY GOD'S WORD MATTERS

SPIRITUAL
Fragrances

XULON ELITE
J. CLARK MELVIN

Xulon Press Elite
2301 Lucien Way #415
Maitland, FL 32751
407.339.4217
www.xulonpress.com

© 2022 by J. Clark Melvin

All rights reserved solely by the author. The author guarantees all contents are original and do not infringe upon the legal rights of any other person or work. No part of this book may be reproduced in any form without the permission of the author.

Due to the changing nature of the Internet, if there are any web addresses, links, or URLs included in this manuscript, these may have been altered and may no longer be accessible. The views and opinions shared in this book belong solely to the author and do not necessarily reflect those of the publisher. The publisher therefore disclaims responsibility for the views or opinions expressed within the work.

Unless otherwise indicated, SScripture quotations taken from the King James Version (KJV) – *public domain*.

Paperback ISBN-13: 978-1-66285-128-5
Ebook ISBN-13: 978-1-66285-129-2

Dedication

This book is dedicated to God the Father, Who gave me His inspiration, stamina, and wherewithal to complete it. Sent the "steering committee" to speak creatively into my spirit. Gave me His words and anointed me for this time! My life is Yours, Lord! Have Your way!

To my family:

Husband
Cliff, I know you just wanted me to complete it! Thank you for believing in me—supporting and funding ☺ ALL my endeavors from the very start, and for allowing me the space to do it! You are my ImprompTWO partner for life! I love you, Honey! – J

Children
Thank you for Championing my cause. Pushing and seemingly harassing me, you know who you are! Lol! ☺ For allowing the creativity of God to flow from Him to me and from me to you all. I love y'all! - Mom

Grandchildren
For always asking me about my book and leaving me alone when I needed to do it, thank you, "stinkies." Love y'all. When I am gone, you'll understand that this was for you – my

children's children. (Sj, Elijah, Melohdi, Noah, and Zoe Anna (Mommy Bear) – you are my heart) -Nahni

To My Family in the Gospel
Uppar Rhoom Ministries, Int'l & Dist. Elder, Pastor, Servant, Mother Ward... only God knows the gratitude that is present. You are the ultimate "steering committee." Thank you for picking up where the ball had been dropped! For taking the time to extract the greatness within – pushing me to greater. Much love! Deaconess and progressing...

To My Father in the Gospel - Pastor Kenneth Hackett: The foundation was laid.

To You, the Reader
Thank you for your supporting efforts, for purchasing and passing the torch to someone else. It means so much! May you be blessed because of it!

So forth and so on... *to everyone, thanks!*
J. Clark Melvin

Table of Contents

Preface xi

SECTION I- FRANKINCENSE & MYRRH

Why Frankincense & Myrrh? 3
Moving Into the Purpose of God 7
In God, There Are NO Options 14
Reduced to the Next Level. 19
You Need an Insecticide: The Word of God Will Do the Job! 33
A Speck 41
It's Uncircumcised – you can do it! 44
Die and Get It Over With 51
Go Limp 62
Kill It! 68
Don't trip – I got this: Grace! .72
You've Got to know it - Prove it - It's Relational 78
Trusting that God Called You! 85
When You Hear the Alarm, Get Up! 87
Look Around and Consider 94
Even in the Darkest Situation, There Is Light. 102
Help Someone Else Get to Jesus. There's more than enough of Him to Go Around 107
What Are You Talkin'? 115
With God, There Is No Guesswork 125

SECTION II- EUCALYPTUS

The Benefits of Eucalyptus? .130

Get a Life! Stop Saying That! 133

Your Life Belongs to God 135
Living In the Moment 138
Released To Perform............................ 140
Wanted but not wanted # got God 142
The Real Deal—Keep It 100 144
Gratefulness................................... 147
What can I say? 149
It Took the Love of God To Do It! 151
Overshadowed To Change The DNA 154
My Way 157
Time - the Appropriator's choice 159
What Day Is It? 162
There's No Such a Thing 163
Are you Offended? 164

SECTION III- LAVENDER

The Reason for Lavender......................... 167
"Heaven has Chosen Me;
So, You Don't Have To!" 169
Time and Purpose 171
Caught... 173
Just do it!..................................... 175
Choices 177
Decide 180
Stupidity: Who is to Blame? 182
Speaking My Heart.............................. 184
Gray Hairs 186
The Birth of a Flower 188
Unchangeable 190
Who Am I? 191
The Pastor's Wife - My Dear Sister 193
Stationary Movement............................ 197
Life Has Meaning 198
My Debut 201

SECTION IV- CYPRESS

When Is CYPRESS Used? 203

Only Remember 205
I've Got This. 207
What a Time! 208

References: 210

Preface

There are many words spoken: only ONE makes the difference. Why does this matter? It matters because words frame; they bring about creative power: good or bad. Have you ever listened to a song, and it dictated your attitude one way or another - changed your persona altogether? Put you in a good place or maybe a negative space. Yes, the music played its own role, but the words worked their way into your spirit – there was an intended purpose! Mission Accomplished.

Words are life… Jesus told His disciples in John 6:63, "…*the words that I speak unto you, they are Spirit, and they are life."* Words have defining power! Case in point, in the beginning, in Genesis chapter one, God's word changed things geographically, environmentally, and atmospherically. He spoke, it happened! What He spoke to - received His words and responded to Them. This indicates the necessity to receive and let productive words attract positive change – lay hold to new life, rather than words to no avail! Whatever comes into your ear gate begins to frame or reframe your existence as it was once known. You have the power to accept or reject, and depending on the content, if rejected, it no longer possesses the ability to create as intended. However, depending on your frame of reference, you will most likely receive it, even if it is over time! Words have sustainability – they linger... *So, the question is, who is sustaining you?*

There are a million books on the market that one can read, but information without the revelation for application is just empty words. How simplistic is it? How refined or refining can it be? Does it bring out the best while revealing the rest? You consider!

When we were children, our parents were the only voices adhered to. They were the gospel – the law. No other voices mattered; regardless, if the truth was spoken, coming from the wrong person, truth was discarded. Our newly programmed voice recognition (response) system, VRS of our parents, governed our thought processes, behaviors, and speech, in most cases! There was no need for anything else - life was good! But, as we began to grow and transform into our own, at the time when the fundamental information that we received should have kicked in like the torque of a sports car merging onto a highway, something else happened. Their voices muted out; other voices (friends, social media, etc.) integrated our Voice Recognition System, and regardless of what we had received, the original VRS no longer carried the same weight! It was debunked and in need of deprogramming.

Although the foundation and essence of life's values remained intact within our database, the new programmers had preeminence. Some maintained what the original VRS downloaded into their databases and thrived and are yet thriving. They went on to become great; doing great things, being impactful with their greatness; and cultivating and extracting the greatness in those around them. Others: succumbed and are yet succumbing to the wiles of the new integration and program in such a way that life is not recognizable. Yet, friends and social media have left the disparity of deciphering what is productive or non-productive. The struggle remains with no hope for an end. So where does this train stop, and you begin? You consider!

Looking at the essence and intent of this book, one can depict this read as a GPS recalculation. Sometimes, we are on course in our travels, but we can easily become turned around. Something about the directions engenders questions that trigger an immediate reaction, which causes a detour from our path - sometimes, maybe an accident. In this process, the GPS will recalculate or reroute, giving a new set of directions to put us on the correct route - we are back on track! Words did it! So, what does that have to do with fragrances: everything – it's accepting or rejecting the recalculation!

We have the same privilege to put on what appeals to us. Sometimes we put on a fragrance to appeal to others. Fragrance is another form of language. It depicts the essence of a mode, an attitude, a purpose; sometimes, excessive fragrances are to mask a hidden or underlying problem. For example, we use well-known air fresheners in our homes to ensure that the smell of whatever does not disturb our guests.

We came up using the disinfectant spray as the room aromatic, but as time progressed, other companies integrated more seemingly pleasant smelling, floral smelling, sweet-smelling, outdoorsy smelling, and whatever else kind of smells that we like. No more is the disinfectant our first choice. Back then, there was no Ralph Lauren's, Coach's, or Chanel's – it is consumer integration that has changed our perspective of smell. Now, we have many options to choose from within one manufacturer. Just as we have the privilege of choosing whose words carry weight in our existence.

There are knock-off fragrances that have marketability and profitability. They have a similar smell to the original, but there is a clear distinction. One must be an avid user to identify the difference. So, what am I saying? Fragrances denote language. We also understand that language consists of words, whether spoken or unspoken. We also know that there are words which we need to adopt, perpetuate, or maybe dismiss. Who chooses which action is necessary?

In the beginning, our parent's words made a difference in our lives. Then other people began to take precedence, changing our course sometimes for the worse. This is the same as with God. He is our Heavenly Parent, the ultimate VRS For life! The same way we accept the integration of others, we should welcome the integration of Him as well.

Sometimes, the words of others resemble the word of the Lord. It looks like it, sounds like it, but the question is: is it? Other words try to parallel themselves with God, but they do not have His stature, weight, or ability to produce the impossible. Consider the cover picture; look at those bottles; what are the similarities? They try to measure up; try to have the same height. There are undeniable similarities that can be deceiving without careful consideration. Without the *"spirit and life"* component, they cannot produce the impossible as God's word can; they remain dormant, having no unction to function.

So, what is it about this book? It is understanding, recognizing, and accepting the ability, purpose, power, passion, progression, plan, and process of The One and Only True God! It is a compilation of words formed to engender thought that produces the desire to be as God intended. That is not to make up our agenda, nor to have it our way like Burger King, but to stay the course that God intended from the very beginning. It isolates and illuminates man's limited choices, despite his perpetual attempt to re-create God's purpose for His subjects.

When Spiritual Fragrances became the title, different aromas immediately came to mind. They are individual writings compiled in sections per their classification, just as we use colognes and perfumes to lavish ourselves and others with the desired essence. We may even use a sweet soft smell in an intimate environment, so we don't stand out like a sore thumb or a sewer system. There are more palatable fragrances that are compelling and alluring when our interest is to reach and appeal to a subject. Some are degenerate and detestable: a preference in which we refrain.

There are scents that can produce an instant headache with excessive smelling. There is floral, and there is sweet; there is earthy, musky, and savory. There are oils that have an aromatic, topical, and ingested effect, with a plethora of health benefits. All these fragrances and aromas have their own flair and place, but who chooses which is appropriate?

This journey into Spiritual Fragrances is to provide you with the wherewithal and necessity of the day, month, year, and lifetime. So, open your nostrils, and receive the breath of life; be quickened and awakened by the engrafted word of God that can save your soul.

Spiritual Fragrance is a realistic depiction of God's word. Put it on and wear it well! Let others smell your essence as you captivate them with His words! In return, you become sweet-smelling if you allow His words to abide in you and you in them. As you continue to accept the word of God and allow its working-power to manifest, you become a fragrant to Him, a sweet-smelling savor in which He delights.

God desires man to maintain the imagery that was put in place. He wants to smell Himself, see Himself, hear Himself, see the reflection of His Son - the Word, as it were from the beginning. Our abiding causes us to receive when we ask of Him; how so, because we ask according to His words that are within us – emanating from our person like a fresh scent!

He is the one fragrance that is universal, and He is acceptable for every occasion.

Read on and enjoy!

SECTION I
FRANKINCENSE & MYRRH
Spiritual Fragrances

Why Frankincense & Myrrh?

Frankincense & Myrrh is used in Spiritual Fragrances because of their representation of the wise.

In the second chapter of the book of Matthew, it is noted that wise men from the East came searching out the King to be born to worship Him – seeing **His** star, which led them to the place where He was. It denotes in verse 11., *"And when they were come into the house, they saw… and fell down and worshipped Him: and when they had opened their treasures, they presented unto Him gifts…"* (KJV). There is no significance about them per se, other than the fact that they were wise in their doings, staying the course and not being rerouted or sidetracked by the deviation that presented itself! You must read the story to understand: Matthew 2nd chapter. It was necessary for them to pursue purpose, and so it is with us.

The scripture says when they saw Him; meaning, when their eyes were opened to Him, a response followed. They fell down; on their knees, on their hands, on their face, it doesn't state, but it does say they worshipped Him. There was an acknowledgment present, an obeisance, a priceless treasure to be released unto Him. They gave what they possessed: Gold, Frankincense, and Myrrh.

Frankincense itself was used as a perfume and spiritual incense, burned in temples throughout the East. It is said to have anti-inflammatory and anti-arthritic properties and has positive effects on the immune system. Frankincense is a "go-to" fragrance when in doubt. Its multi-faceted capabilities are refreshingly noted as being all-purposed.

Myrrh was a sacred anointing oil used to embalm – for death and burial. It has medicinal purposes for healing wounds, digestive health (your processing system), and providing that overall balance. Myrrh has also been used to slow bleeding (when life cuts you, you can apply Myrrh). "Myrrh oil has powerful cleansing properties, especially for the mouth and throat." Keep your breath smelling fresh. Words are fragrances! Frankincense and Myrrh are of great value with a costly price point, used medicinally and to profit. What price has been paid for you?

Frankincense was said to acknowledge Jesus' priesthood – setting Him apart from other kings. It represents exclusivity and distinction. In Spiritual Fragrances, this distinction carries the same connotation. When Frankincense and Myrrh are applied to the matters of our heart, healing can begin; it soothes and is applied as a purifier. Jesus received and has given what is required for a life of fulfillment.

As these men from the East, we will also be considered wise when we allow God to lavish us with this effervescence that has healing properties and wholeness. What God intends for us to put on is of great price.

What's your treasure?

But He said unto them, I have meat to eat that ye know not of." John 4:32 (KJV)

"Jesus saith unto then, My meat is to do the will of Him that sent me, and to finish His work." John 4:34 (KJV)

"In all thy ways acknowledge Him, and He shall direct thy paths." Proverbs 3:6 (KJV)

"Those things, which ye have both learned, and received, and heard, and seen in me do: and the God of peace shall be. With you." Philippians 4:9 (KJV)

Moving Into the Purpose of God

Just like those wise men from the East, I am certain they had no real idea what they were doing. But they were inspired to do it and continued in it, until they reached their destination. There was a universal compass given to them, something of which they obviously were familiar: His star.

Remarkably enough, the scripture says, they came asking, *"Where is He that is born King... for we have seen His star in the East, and are come to worship Him."* Whether three, thirty, three hundred, or three thousand, these men had the right idea; they came to worship. But how is it they followed His star? Wait a minute, for that matter; to whom did they ask this question, and where did this notion about a King born come from?

The text doesn't indicate how far from the east was it to Bethlehem that they travelled, and regardless of this point, they travelled from afar to worship what was only an inclination. They had no real proof or knowledge of it; they came to discover the truth. They were in pursuit of it – the truth that was in their hearts.

Some would say that we don't have enough information to say so, but I say, whether they were astrologers (people who studied the stars) or magicians, they had some information that was supernatural. It was clear these men moved into the purpose of God.

It doesn't indicate that they were of the Christian faith; as a matter of fact, Astrology is far removed from what would be considered Christian. In this case, it really didn't matter; God had a plan and gave them access to it by way of their familiarity: stars.

The implication here is this; one doesn't have to know what one is doing. God will use the familiar to bring one to a place where He is glorified, and His purpose can be revealed. One must trust His move and move.

What was it with these dudes? They had a small infraction with King Herod that did not stop them. Herod also had been given a heads up that something was about to go down! The word will always get around when God is up to something. You can rest assured that if there is a plan in motion, there is a plan to impede that motion too!

The wise men from the East and King Herod sought for He that is born King, but for separate reasons. Although King Herod desired to destroy Jesus because he felt he was a threat to his kingdom, God's plan was to destroy Herod. Everyone involved with Jesus' birth had an active role in the purpose of God: from Mary to Joseph, to the wise men, and even to Herod that sought to kill Him. The aim is for purpose, and sometimes it appears that what is purpose is not really God's purpose, as it would seem in this case. Oh, but it was!

Moving into the purpose of God is likened unto the same for everyone. One really doesn't know anything about where, how, what, when, or who. The important piece is that one hears, perceives, and obeys, regardless of knowledge or the lack thereof. There must be a willingness to adhere to what God is doing, even if it seems strange!

What has been gathered here about the process of moving from these men of the East? One, it's important not to concern oneself with the details that belong to God. Two, God may use what is familiar to a person to execute His plan. Three, the attitude toward the assignment is equally important as the assignment. Four, if there is no knowledge of what is to be done, ask somebody. Five, do not let the distractions encountered become obstacles. Six, if the course deviates for any reason, get back on track! Seven, recognize Who it is that is being sought out! Eight, don't hate – celebrate and worship Him. And Nine, the treasure that is opened up is specific and of great value.

So, what is it to move? It is to go in a specific direction or manner; change positions/directions; it is a controlled action - movement. Purpose: is the reason for which something is done, created, or for which something exists. Is it safe to say these folks didn't really have the full understanding; however, the wise men were onto something. I guess that's why they were known as wise men.

Moving in God's purpose is always contrary to us. It forces us to take the exit out of ourselves, which is the only way to go there. Well, one might ask, "what is God's purpose?" Wasn't it just stated that it is not always known right away; one must recognize when opportunities arise for one to do the opposite of what is the norm?

To say one needs to move is to imply that placement was not intact from the beginning. Whether it was a wander away from what was originally purposed or just having no clue at all, one must move away from their own source of effort, strength, will, and off one's own course.

Just like driving on the road, not paying attention to the path, or what is intended for that matter, will cause a veering off to the left or right and possibly ending in someone else's lane. How can this be fixed? By coming to oneself and moving into the purposed lane.

One might ask, what does this look like? One can't answer exactly, but it can be surmised that moving into the purpose of God may be out of one's scope of knowledge, influence, ability, understanding, and comfort on the outside of self. Often, one becomes complacent or drawn by the comforts they have known. While there is a transition moving into a new place, a new season, a new year, it's equally important not to delete God from the move.

Proverbs 3:5-6, specifically indicates that acknowledgement and trust in God will cause Him to direct paths. Isn't that the objective – to be led? Sometimes when the move is outside of the purpose of God, the location and destination become foreign. Focus must be like unto those men, who had every reason to move away from their assignment, but diligence and commitment to the assignment offered them an opportunity to reset, and they took it! Back on target!

There is never an opportunity that doesn't present itself to make a change. God wouldn't be true to His Word if there was no way of escape: the EXIT sign is always illuminated. God has given everyone the same opportunities within the scope of their reference. Moving into purpose is the recognition of the current season with the willingness to operate in it: that is the critical value here.

The odds up against don't matter because God gives the grace to move, just as He did to those wise men from the East. He directs, anoints, and provides resources while moving. As the Global Positioning System, a.k.a. GPS, recalculates when one is off course, God does the same; He recalculates. The beautiful thing is that God's purpose is not of men. There is no disappointment in God – the destination is sure.

During the transition into this new unknown, never seen before year – it is a prime opportunity to move into what God has purpos__ed__. The "ed" on purpose represents the past tense of purpose. It is the already established reason. It is the why one exists. God didn't leave it up to man to figure out; one just needs to say "Yes!"

So, whatever God speaks - do! Move into what He originally said. Don't be influenced by surroundings but allow Him to be the influence that will propel and guarantee a safe arrival to destiny. What is it that He can use? Remember that God looks on the heart, not the outward appearance of a thing. See what God's purpose is concerning the matter and get back onto the original lane intended like those wise men did. First, recognize this,

Destination is His expectation:
1. Recognize one doesn't know the way
2. Accept the fact that there was a deviation from the course.
3. Allow Him to recalculate a fresh start if He wills.
4. Illumination is God's business. The requirement is for one to walk therein.

And so it is for this incoming new season; move! If the question is, what does that look like? Ask Him!

"Jesus saith unto them, My meat is. To do the will of Him that sent Me, and to finish His work." John 4:34 (KJV)

"Then answered Jesus and said unto them, Verily, verily, I say unto you, The Son can do nothing of Himself, but what He seeth the Father do: for what things soever He doeth, these also doeth the Son likewise." John 5:19 (KJV)

"For I came down from heaven, not to do mine own will, but the will of Him that sent me." John 6:38 (KJV)

5."Trust in the Lord with all thine heart; and lean not unto thine own understanding. 6.In all thy ways acknowledge Him, and He shall direct thy paths." Proverbs 3:5-6 (KJV)

In God, There Are NO Options

The song was pinned: "He didn't have to do it, but He did!" On the contrary, it was His meat to do the will of the Father; He had to – He wanted to – He did!

Culturally, we came up with these songs, and we grow up singing them, teaching our children to sing them - our children's children… we perpetuate error. Now, you may say, how so? I'm glad you asked. Jesus' purpose was to do the will of Him, Who sent Him. He didn't have a choice – whether He would redeem man. Didn't God already plan this? If Jesus was/is the Word, then this talk was what He was/is – right? It's His Word! How then did the choice of doing something different come into play? With that in mind, how did He have His own mind? If we are admonished to have the mind of Christ, when does our unsaved and sinful mind come into play? It doesn't.

Jesus came to restore the Father's work that man and the devil altered through disobedience. Lucifer betrayed God in heaven and was cast down to the earth where he became what we know him as now, Satan and the Devil (Isaiah 14:12). God made what Lucifer was cast down into, the earth. It was a place of nothing. God had a plan and began to frame it by His words. So, He spoke everything into place and set man in the midst of it; Satan, the devil, was there too!

Man, and God had a thing going on... they were one in Spirit. So, here is my theory: God cast Lucifer out into a place of nothing, and by the Words of God, a portrait of splendor was designed with Satan, the Devil, in the midst of it all. You can't avoid your surroundings; you've got to deal with them! Although Satan is in the midst, what God made was good!

Lucifer was a beautiful spirit-being when God began to make this and that. After being cast down, He charged the serpent amid the garden, just as he did that herd of swine in the country of the Gadarenes (Mark 5:1). He had everything when he was with God but one thing: options. He wanted something else; to be someone else; he wanted to be God. He wasn't satisfied with the position that he had, the make-up that God ordained him to have; he wanted more; he wanted God's place.

Now, according to Genesis 2nd chapter, Adam was made by the hand of God, and His life-giving breath entered his being and caused activity, a lifeless soul to live. Beauty was all around him, except that there was something missing: no help and companionship – another potential option (that's another time and place, let's stay on task). God gave him help and companionship too and charged them to keep what He said, to eat freely of every tree in the garden except of the Tree of the Knowledge of good and evil (verse 17). See, the option was laced inside of the command: good and evil – eat of every tree except this specific one. God did not intend for man to use or have options for that matter, but man determined to have what he wanted: options. This was the seed of Lucifer, as he was transforming into Satan through pride.

God is a Spirit. Although Man is too, he was clothed with an outer layer that could be seen. He wrapped him in skin clothes and placed him in the midst of the garden for a purpose to execute. He had a purpose, and that was his final job. God made everything for man to have pleasure in. It was never for man to experience hardship; if it were so, I believe that God would have spoken it that way from the beginning (see Genesis 1:26-28). What man had was God's absolute best! Remember, God never constructs a plan that He does not intend to execute or provide for. It's never frivolous, and it's always top-notch!

So, what happened? Man was presented the option to disobey God, from the father of division. Instead of maintaining his space, he lost his place; why, because of options. This is the one area where man continues to fail, and that is in eliminating options, particularly when it comes to God. Division is not of God! A house divided against itself cannot stand (Mark 3:25 emphasized) You honor Me with your lips, but your heart is far from Me (Matthew 15:8 emphasized). Can you see the parallel options? There are no oxymorons to glean from or contrast to adopt here. You can't do good bad. Consider that you cannot have two masters, God and the Devil.

Sometimes He does give choices; for example: "...I have set before you life and death..." Deuteronomy 30:19 and "...chose you this day whom ye will serve..." Joshua 24:15. But really, the commandment is clear; He says, "...therefore chose life, that both thou and thy seed may live." The option is wrapped in disobedience. Other generations lack and fail because of the inability to be steadfast in what He said. The blessing of the Lord that makes rich is forfeited because of options, and here comes the sorrow. Proverbs 10:22

We must recall and live by knowing that God's intention is not optional; after all, it's intentional. In God, there are no options, no choices – it's His way or no way exists!

Amen!

"For whosoever will save his life shall lose it: but whosoever will lose his life for my sake, the same shall save it." Luke 9:24 (KJV)

"Therefore whosoever heareth these sayings of mine, and doeth them, I will liken him unto a wise man, which built his house upon a rock". Matthew 7:24 (KJV)

Reduced to the Next Level

The oxymoron

This will sound much like a contradiction to my statement in "In God, There Are No Options" …that there are no oxymorons in God. But you must understand the concept of thought here. Hot and Cold don't exist together. Light and dark don't happen at the same time. Good and bad do not coexist. So, when I said you can't do good bad, this is an accurate statement, so let's proceed.

Only in God, by His power, do these contrasts exist. "My strength is made perfect in weakness. Most gladly, therefore, will I rather glory in my infirmities… when I am weak, then am I strong." II Corinthians 12 chapter. The implication that infirmities engender the power of Christ resting on is absurd to man. Humanly, this doesn't even make sense… it's not logical, but in Christ Jesus, all things are possible through Him. So, what are we saying? You can only produce these contrasts in God at His discretion. Are we clear? I sure hope so!

While reading Judges 7:1-7, I discovered some pivotal points of interest; life lessons that led to victory according to the scriptures. Often, we take the literal concept of the Word of God only and do not seek to receive the unspoken word beyond the pages of life. Let us look closer.

As we read the first verse together. Let's quickly walk through this!

> Verse 1. *"Then Jerrubbaal, who is Gideon, and all the people that were with him, rose up early and pitched beside the well of Harod: so that the host of the Midianites were on the northside of them by the hill of Moreh, in the valley."*

There are some pivotal points inside this one verse. Gideon had another name... another identity. He also had influence - enough for it to be noted that there were people with him. One getting up early to do a thing reflects a crucial value to success. Sometimes... one must have a specific target, a specified location/destination; you just can't be loosey-goosey going with the flow of everything. Another point shows how positioning themselves where the enemy is concerned is strategic and important every time for victory to be warranted. Focus is the priority. How about the importance of them being together?

There are cliches that depict this truth, like "Birds of a feather flock together" and "Association brings assimilation." The bible asks, "Can two walk together, except they be agreed?" Amos 3:3 (KJV) How is this possible if one walks North and the other South; there is no productivity here. The outcome is never what is expected because of division.

Let's just talk about us; when we are together, our speech is the same, our goal(s) to which we have agreed to agree is the same, and so is our timing. There is also a necessity to get an early start on whatever we embark upon. It allots time for preparation, strategy, human error, and perhaps unforeseen circumstances. Implementation is critical; we must do it together and do it right early. The Word of the Lord is mandatory on any matter for the victory to be won! Don't leave home without it. And that's just it.

The precursor to this story is the conversation between the Angel of the Lord and Gideon (Judges 6th chapter). Why was there a conversation to start? Because of those Midianites and the rest of the crew, who kept stealing what they had gained. Isn't it disheartening to work for something or have been given something, and some bully comes and "takes the lunch money?" ...Such a violation of one's character. This is why Gideon was hiding his wheat in the first place, trying to maintain what he had. Wow, that's another story altogether, but it is exactly what we do; so very familiar with abuse, the misuse, the rejection, denial, and theft that we acquiesce every chance we get to hide what God gave us. Sometimes we will not let others see, let alone know what is in us; neither will we let them know what we can do for fear of exploitation.

God had given Israel over into the hand of the Midianites because of the evil they did in His sight. He let those Midianites prevail for seven years until His word was sent to Gideon. The cry of God's people moved His compassion to deliver them. Cry loud! God sent a prophet to speak to the people, thus saith the Lord. He reminded them of the victories He's won. Read it for yourself: the 6th chapter of Judges.

After the prophet spoke to the people, God sent the Angel to speak to the man: the one whom God chose to lead out His victory. Why was the prophet's word not enough? Have any idea? God needed to bring about an agreement so that they could do it together.

Gideon's perspective of himself was off. One would say he had low self-esteem; I say he had pride. His focus was on himself and what he could not do, isn't that self-exaltation, self-consumption, self-mutilation, etc.? It indeed was centered around "self." He apparently forgot Who had the victory; some way or another, Gideon mixed this thing up! Did he think he was going to do it? He must have, by the way, he had addressed the Angel of the Lord. Talk about hidden conceit. One must look closely to see this. Let's speed up our reading.

After Gideon's shenanigans with the Angel trying to prove God, he finally received what was being said about him and God's desire to deliver by way of his hand, which brings us here. The people and Gideon were now together, there was an agreement to free themselves, and God was going to do it. But a proving process was necessary: a process of elimination. Let's parallel this to now. Whoever is with us must be on board with the program that we've been tasked to do. There cannot be a fight over rank, personality, or authority. We must be fitly joined together and compacted by that which every joint supplies (that is His Spirit), according to the effectual working… Ephesians

4:16, we must be together AND work effectively. We have to position ourselves… if our enemy is pursuing us, we ought to pursue him also. Read on!

> Verse 2. *"And the Lord said unto Gideon, the people that are with thee are too many for Me to give the Midianites into their hands, lest Israel vaunt themselves against Me, saying, Mine own hand hath saved me." Judges 7:2 (KJV)*

What! Did God not know how many entities were bullying them? Did He not see what was going on? Did He not know that they were going to get whooped! If they could have whooped the Midianites, they would not have permitted their substance to be confiscated in the first place – right? This sounds like pride again, as if they were going to win their own battle: Not!

First, we can't hear Him without relationship: a posture of submission and agreement. We should always have an open ear to hear God and to do what was heard. Relationships are critical to one's ability to hear, receive, do, and succeed. (Joshua 1:8 KJV).

Next, we must be apt to receive what He is saying, even when it doesn't make sense to us. Who do we think we are, that the God of everything needs to make sense to… us? We want Him to make sense, though! See, we must accept that the Lord is doing this! What do the people have to do with it other than reaping the harvest that God has sown – Nothing? This is God's victory! There is much consolation in this thought! If it is The Lord's doing, then it is sure to be so!

Also, the Lord recognizes the possibilities of us taking His glory! He knows where we are when we don't know. He may reduce us so that we understand that our ability did none of this! Our wherewithal, our wit, our might, our knowledge, our strength, our connections had nothing in this! Neither was it any good of our own, but it was/is the Lord's doing. We've got to know that it is not us but God. The key is how He chooses to reduce. That Self-Righteousness has got to go, lest we forget!

> *Verse 3. "Now, therefore, go to proclaim in the ears of the people saying, whosoever is fearful and afraid, let him return and depart early from Mount Gilead...."*

There are those things that are identified that cannot be with us in the battle for souls. Can we identify a few things? Our wherewithal, our wit, our might, our knowledge, our strength, our connections, our insight, our feelings, our perspective, our desire, our ambitions, even our family – none of it! Drop it all off! (Figuratively speaking)

God sends a word to us for recognition of those things that are illegal immigrants, aliens, fugitives, and trespassers to the promise. It's amazing how we understand all these words in the natural, but in the spirit, we cannot recognize them in ourselves. Is it the respect of persons?

God called out fear because that is a factor for many believers, people in general. But now, the world promotes satanism and horror in such a way that we must look at other things among fear.

Fear and being afraid are part of our emotional bank. We know that our emotions have a way of telling on us. They know just how to expose us; no matter how much we try to keep our composure; our emotions will find us out - for all to see! He did give us fear, but not the spirit of fear (II Tim. 1:7). So how many fears are there? There is reverential, and there is being afraid and fearful because of influence. What is He referring to here: fear and being afraid.

And the Bible said, *"...And there returned of the people twenty-two thousand: and there remained ten thousand."*

Of all that were present, only a smidgen remained, just by identifying one aspect of weight: fear. It was one-third left to be exact.

So, we know that there were a lot of people initially present, but the number of them was too many, and God was not willing to do what He wanted to do with the multitude. Why? Because of the unknown weakness.

Sometimes, it's just too much flesh! God is unwilling to do in us what He desires because of it! **Declare IT WITH ME - FLESH, YOU'VE GOT TO GO!**

Even after He reduced them down by twenty-two thousand, there were still ten thousand folks left. It was a substantial smidgen to work with.

> *Verse 4. "And the Lord said unto Gideon. The people are yet too many; bring them down unto the water:"*

Tell yourself - It's still too much!

He commanded Gideon to bring the people to a specific place. It was a place of trying, a place of testing, a place where it was proven what manner of men they were.

God has a way of bringing out what is in us. We can't hide the goods from God. To Him, we are sponges whom when He squeezes, one can see what has saturated! And He tells Gideon, you don't have to do anything, *"...and I will try them for thee there:"*

Now, look at that! He would try them for him! God wants to identify the mess on our behalf, to rid us of the contraband! We need not do anything but obey God. In other words, if God says to us that we've got to get rid of this and get rid of that, it is no longer an option if we want to progress in Him and have the victory.

"...and it shall be that of whom I say unto thee this shall go with thee, the same shall go with thee; and of whomsoever, I say unto thee, this shall not go with thee, the same shall not go."

Again, it is identification. It is the shaking of those things that could not be shaken so that what remains is permissible and purposed. It is the loose him and let him go moment! We must be willing to release! Sometimes, we become accustomed to our nature, and we find God's nature restrictive: exactly!

So, with that, God allows the trials to come; He will enable those tests, He will allow the dilemma to arise in our lives – taking us to another facet of proving if need be! God and others are watching to see just how we deal with circumstances. Remember, this is our proving ground – what manner of man we are. So, our response is crucial to determine if we are ready to go to the next realm in the Spirit. But our flesh must die! That's where we are!

> *Verse 5. "So he brought down the people unto the water and the Lord said unto Gideon, everyone that lappeth of the water with his tongue, as a dog lappeth, him shall thou set by himself; likewise every one that boweth down upon his knees to drink water.*

So, God told Gideon what to look for in the people. We, too, must recognize and accept what God shows us about who and what goes with us in the service of the Lord. We can't trip because God is ridding us of and rooting us out! He told him the specific attribute to look for. God is explicit, and when we are serious, He identifies this attribute to us by speaking directly, not parabolic, but directly.

What is highlighted? Here's this test. The Lord is looking at us, and He is saying, "If your flesh jumps out, if you are disorderly, if you act inappropriately; even if you have the respect of persons, if you are slow to hear - quick to speak, quick to be angry. If you strive, if you envy, if you covet, if you backbite, if you are merciless, if you sow discord among the brethren, if you can't bridle your tongue, if you're disobedient, if you're not faithful, if you are selfish, self-centered, self-righteous, if you are an adulterer in the natural or in the spirit, if you are a fornicator in the natural or the spirit, if you have malice and have lust; if you are an idolater, and/or rebellious; if you see any of these traits and/or the like, then, some more of your flesh will have to go! Oh, my goodness, there will be none of me left! "Yes, that's right!" Saith the Lord

> *Verse 6. "And the number of them that lapped, putting their hand to their mouth, were three hundred men: but all the rest of the people bowed down upon their knees to drink water."*

Look at these odds! This is a drastic decrease! This looks like a place of defeat! There is no way victory can come by way of this small number! These people are too large for us! There is not enough to take on an army of anything! We are no more individuals; it's as if we have lost ourselves! All these thoughts and feelings flood our soul; because it's not saved, our spirit is redeemed. However, mass reduction is necessary. God is re-calling the defective product to rid us of hazards and casualties.

When we are reduced to the place of use, His strength is made perfect in our weakness. Our reduction enables us to say, "His grace is sufficient for us: then, we can experience an elevation in God, where His strength is made perfect in weakness.

> *Verse 7. "And the Lord said unto Gideon, By the three hundred that lapped will I save you, and deliver the Midianites into thine hand..."*

The Lord said, by this reduction in character, person, attitude, behavior, instinct, intuition, I can now deliver and save! The significant reduction didn't seem necessary to the natural eye, but it was to God - it was His plan of redemption. Jesus, being one man, saved the world. It was not His disciples or those who followed afar off, but one man saved the day, and that is the same way He must reduce us down until there is very minimal of us: at best, none of us.

Now, He can keep reducing us down and down until there is no more existence of us, period, physically either. *Isaiah 64:6 says, "...all of our righteousness are as filthy rags." I John 5:17a says, "All unrighteousness is sin...." Romans 6:23a says, "For the wages of sin is death...!"* So, if He continues to reduce us down and down and down because of our sinful nature, there would not be any more existence of us, period, <u>but had it not been for His grace!</u>

Romans 5:20 & 21 says, "Moreover the law entered that the offense might abound. But where sin abounded, grace did much more abound: that as sin hath reigned unto death, even so might grace reign through righteousness unto eternal life by Jesus Christ our Lord." (KJV)

So, the more messed up we are, the more <u>grace</u> is extended. Now, that doesn't mean that we go and deliberately mess up because we get more grace, but peradventure, we do mess up – grace is given regardless of worth!

So, it is when God is enabled by our volition to have total control of our lives that we can really demonstrate His power. This is when we can really experience triumphant living, abundant living, victorious living; and this is where deliverance can really begin for us and for others.

God has a desire to process and progress us in the kingdom. *Luke 12:32 says, "Fear not little flock, for it is your Father's good pleasure to give you the kingdom."* He wants to give us everything that He has, but as we currently stand, He can't do His will because our flesh is "out of control!"

I remember a church sister said that the Lord told her that we had to "whip those demons" in our lives. Until we do that, we can't experience moving to progressive levels in God. He can't trust us with His "unleashed and absolute power." He can't even depend on us to control our own flesh. And most often, it's our attitudes; we must learn how to rule our spirit.

Proverbs 25:28 says, "He that hath no rule over his own spirit is like a city that is broken down, and without walls." The word says, if we can't have rule over our own spirit, we are just busted up and disgusted, we don't even have a clue of who we really are, and we are all over the place. When there are no walls, anything can come in; anything can shake us, so we must rule our own spirit, our spirit, and not somebody else's.

Proverbs 16:32 says, "He that is slow to anger is better than the mighty; he who rul<u>eth</u> (meaning continues to rule) his spirit than he that taketh a city." The Bible says we are powerful, and we are strong, and there is nothing that we won't be able to do; God can really use us at this point. And it is until we respond according to the word and do what God expects and commands us to do - we cannot, we won't move to

the next level in Him. We will not experience the victories that He intended for us to experience. God is a disciplinarian and a stickler on principle. Therefore, He will chastise His sons. So, when we find that God is continuously showing and telling us how much of our flesh is in the way, we ought to be excited that He loves us that much.

Hebrews 12:11-13 says, [11] *"Now no chastening for the present seemeth to be joyous, but grievous: nevertheless, afterwards it yieldeth the peaceable fruit of righteousness unto them which are exercised thereby.* ¹². *Wherefore lift up the hands which hang down, and the feeble knees;* ¹³. *And make straight paths for your feet, lest that which is lame be turned out of the way, but let it rather be healed."*

We must let the Lord reduce us so that we can go on in victory. Recognize and accept that what we have left over is exactly what God requires to fight and be victorious – all of us won't work! Don't fight against God, but for Him. Let Him work the work in us. So Yes, God will have to reduce us, so He can take us to the next level.

"For the word of God is quick, and powerful, and sharper than any two-edged sword, piercing even to the dividing asunder of soul and spirit, and of the joints and marrow, and is a discerner of the thoughts and intents of the heart." Hebrews 4:12 (KJV)

"Then said Jesus unto his disciples, If any man will come after me, let him deny himself, and take up his cross, and follow me." Matthew 16:24 (KJV)

"And he said to them all, If any man will come after me, let him deny himself, and take up his cross daily, and follow me." Luke 9:23 (KJV)

"And he said to them all, If any man will come after me, let him deny himself, and take up his cross daily, and follow me." Mark 8:34 (KJV)

You Need an Insecticide: The Word of God Will Do the Job!

The Lord gave me an interesting analogy about bugs, particularly because I had an outbreak of bugs in my house many years ago. It wasn't because I had bugs when I first moved in, but when the <u>next-door neighbors came/moved</u> in…the bugs came too!

Hmm, as I proofed this writing, I got a different angle; when the neighbors came, the bugs showed up! What is that? Don't allow other people's circumstances or situations to be the source of your problem. You must man your space! Let's go on…

Once I saw enough bugs in odd places, and at odd times, I realized that there was a problem on the rise, <u>and if I did nothing about it, it would quickly escalate beyond control</u>. Recognize what is being contributed versus what you are bringing to the table. You are involved in the process with a responsibility one-way or the other.

There are certain indicators that identify what type of bug case you have; the PCO-Pest Control Operators will ask:

1. Are they in the Bathroom?

The place of intimacy, particularly behind the toilet, indicates they are coming through the pipes, an inside job.

2. What about the Kitchen?

Place where constant activity and carelessness of leaving things out easily takes place.

3. Have you seen them outside?

Indicating it's an outside job; they are traveling seeking rest. You have to cut them off to stop the process.

4. How many have you seen?

Identifies the intensity of infestation and how bad is the problem. Never underestimate it!

He even looked around to see what kind of house I kept because that is important too! How do you keep your house? As a matter of fact, how do you keep the house, the temple of the Spirit of God?

These questions are key questions that help them decipher how to deal with the problem. Without knowledge of these, the problem becomes a bit more complicated; however, it can be addressed, perhaps by the process of elimination.

It is always important to locate the origin if you can because then, you can go directly to the source of the matter, but if you have no idea, it will prolong the process almost always! What is your problem? When did it start?

While I was praying, the Lord gave me this illustration of <u>how evil comes</u> into people's lives. Most times, for sane people anyhow, they don't just simply invite bugs/evil, but in some kind of way, "they" the bugs/evil get in. I say they because <u>nothing shows up a singular; it's always in the plural, in groups.</u>

He showed me <u>that once you see the problem, you'd need to make the call</u>. But originally, I did not call; I <u>tried to deal with the problem myself</u> by buying spray, traps, and boric acid. I had a lot of things that were on the market, but <u>was any of them effective</u>? Needless to say, I continued to see bugs here and there. And that's just it; we think we can handle stuff ourselves. Not realizing this is a professional's job! He Who knows.

These bugs are smart; they've been around a while; they are survivors, ready to do whatever they need to do to live, even if it's in your house—they are seeking rest. This is their objective to invade your space – to take over, lay claims to what's yours!

The Lord showed me that the <u>only effective way to treat a bug problem was by calling on the Insecticide Officer to come and administer treatment.</u> When he came, <u>he let me know what he was going to do, where he was going to target</u> even if I didn't see any, and <u>possibly how many times it would take</u> to resolve the issue. He even let me know <u>what the intensity of the problem</u> for me was…

all of this was done on the first visit. If you listen to what is being said the first time, you'll be better off!

He also told me not to be alarmed if, after he left, I began to <u>start seeing more of them come out.</u> He said, "This is a good thing; that means that they can take the insecticide back to the others, and they too will die, <u>and it's working.</u>" We need to have the same attitude of the bugs, to invade and infect their territory.

Needless to say, I did see more, and of course, I panicked because I had never seen that many; it didn't mean that they were not there, it just meant that I did not see them myself, but they were present. Sometimes, we have things going on in our lives, and we feel that it is a minor thing at first until the Human Pest Inspector comes into the scheme. And <u>until the inspector came, I had never seen them in that magnitude.</u> Which reminded me of the scripture in **Psalm 119:130, which says, "The entrance of Thy word giveth light; it giveth understanding unto the simple."** <u>Until the light of the word was ushered in, requested to come, called upon, nothing could take place!</u>

Even after the Inspector came, I still saw bugs here and there; I even saw some dead in strange places. But it took several occasions of his coming before I started to see the results. Because I had no idea how bad my problems were internally and/or externally, I underestimated the dilemma and the need to resolve it. I seemed to have <u>allowed it to linger;</u> until it was beyond recognition and control for me.

Before the inspector left, he mentioned what my responsibility was in this equation; I needed to always make sure things were clean; that's why he noted what type of house I kept from the beginning. He could identify what type of job he was up against depending on how I kept my house. Had I been a nasty housekeeper, his job would have been horrendous, but careful notation caused him to briefly list what was needed.

Always make sure things are clean.

Never leave anything on the floor, dog food, crumbs, and things of that sort!

And they loved paper; *loose* paper lying around was not a good thing.

So, he let me know that there were things that I was going to have to do in order to aid in the rid of this problem.

So, what am I saying? There are times when things show up at our house – the house of our soul, in our vessels, and we have no idea how they got there. This evil messes up our lives and the lives of those around us; we must do something about it! The problem is that we think we can do something without God, and we begin to assess the issue. We get advice from people, things, books, from whatever seeking resolution; when all we have to do is call the insecticide operator, which is, in this case, The Word of God.

In that same Psalm 119:130 says *the entrance of... indicating it's been called in, requested, summoned, invited to come; there must first be an invitation to make an entrance.* Is this always? Yes! Nothing can enter without an invitation! Invitation can sometimes be indirect. Have you ever ended up with someone at your house because you said the wrong thing, and it seemed like an invitation to them? That's how we invite without inviting, and instead of coming right out and saying no thank you, we go along with it, tolerating it, which leads us to trouble and frustration; and now you have someone at your house that we really didn't want there.

The same is it for evil. We don't just say evil come and visit, but it shows up when Sister So&So doesn't help where needed; we let evil remain. We do not address evil because we feel the sister was inconsiderate and selfish, so we magnify all those feelings about her. Now, is evil showing up uninvited, or did the nasty attitude invite him? And now he's brought aggravation, confusion, complaining, backbiting, wrath, and the rest of the clan. Trying to deal with evil on your own is a long process. Had we been able to deal with evil, evil would not have been present in the first place.

We need the entrance of the word of God in our lives to bring results. The bug problem of sin doesn't just go away; something has to be done about it! We have to make the call on the Word. When the word comes according to **John 15:3 "Now ye are clean through the word which I have spoken unto you."** It is not until the word comes that anything can be cleaned.

So, what are we going to do about this problem? There is only one call to make! Do it today for free; it's an already paid in full presentation! We play a role in this…we must keep our house. We can't afford to be ashamed to make the call because we have unwanted visitors in our spirit. We can get them out if we want to! Follow instructions. Keep our places tidied up, not leaving excess things out for those critters to nibble on. *(Neither give place to the Devil. Ephesians 4:27)*

Flesh caters to the bugs of our soul! Only the Word of God can illuminate the problem, and in many instances, bring them to the forefront, all to be done away with… but we have to make the call. Call today!

"And ye shall know the truth, and the truth shall make you free." John 8:32 (KJV)

"Howbeit when He, the Spirit of Truth, is come, He will guide you into all truth... and He will shew you things to come." John 16:13 (KJV)

"For as many as are led by the Spirit of God, they are the sons of God." Romans 8:14 (KJV)

"This I say then, walk in the Spirit, and ye shall not fulfill the lust of the flesh." Galatians 5:16 (KJV)

"Beloved, believe not every spirit, but try the spirits whether they are of God..." I John 4:1 (KJV)

A Speck

The Spirit of God is our compass. What is the purpose of a compass? "A compass is a device that indicates direction. It is one of the most important instruments for navigation and is mainly used on off-road terrain.

People use it to find their way, which indicates they do not know where to go or how to get back to civilization. With this tool, one always has the guarantee of knowing how to go back if things go awry." The Spirit of God is our compass. He governs where to go regardless of the good or bad; He is our guide.

We must become quite sensitive to the Spirit of God. We do not have to figure out what is going on within an element. The Spirit can identify what is required if we are sensitive and trust His leading.

We understand that sensitivity does not exist independently. One is susceptible to a thing, but what is that thing? So, how do we become sensitive to the Spirit of God? It is brought about with constant exposure!

Saturation creates a molecular sense to or of a thing. We must be saturated with the things of God. Everything about us must be God-driven, God-induced, God-ordained, God-invoked, God-provoked. We cannot intermingle with any other being to include self/flesh. There must be a renouncing of our person to receive the pureness of God's Spirit. We must trust what God is saying and/or doing in a thing.

Often, we reject what the Spirit of God presents to us because we gravitate to the familiar. Sometimes, it is the form of. God needs to reveal the blemishes in the Spirit by seeing through the eye of His Spirit. It is Discerning of Spirits - contrary to what the human eye sees; it is the truth.

The sensitivity of His Spirit becomes quite tasking because of what we know and receive. He does not flow with the direction of our current. We must be willing to do and go according to the will of God and not allow knowledge to overcharge us. God cover us! We want God to illuminate whatever and anything that needs to be seen. Can we handle it? That's why the upgrade is necessary.

In our first state, we cannot handle what we see because it will be in its purest form - unfiltered. Lord, prepare me! We desire to be used by God but are still babes. He is looking to mature us quickly. No fear, no doubt, no unbelief, and no intimidation—just obedience. We can't fall for the tactic of intimidation. It is to shut us down, to distort our vision! We must know what we are seeing, and to know is to discern the spirit by way of His Spirit: the compass. We cannot discern by the flesh; this is where the distortion enters. God is not the author of confusion. We must know His word; see the speck and let Him reveal the finite.

"These things I have spoken unto you, that in me ye might have peace. In the world ye shall have tribulation: but be of good cheer: I have overcome the world." -John 16:33 (KJV)

"And when they began to sing and to praise, the LORD set ambushments against the children of Ammon, Moab, and Mount Seir, which were come against Judah; and they were smitten." II Chronicles 20:22 (KJV)

[50.] "So David prevailed over the Philistine with a sling and with a stone, and smote the Philistine, and slew him; but there was no sword in the hand of David. [51.] Therefore David ran, and stood upon the Philistine, and took his sword, and drew it out of the sheath thereof and slew him, and cut off his head therewith." I Samuel 17:50-51 (KJV)

It's Uncircumcised – you can do it!

Uncircumcised – why on earth would anyone want to outwardly discuss this subject? It is what happens to the male factors - the life-giving gender. It is the cutting away of…. Of what? The excess skin that overlaps the head of the male penis. This skin is a hazard and can cause great infections to both males and females during intimacy. This overlap harnesses bacterium if not properly cared for: cleaned and well dried off.

This uncircumcision has a peculiar look. I imagine that it can project a particular foul smell when infected or unclean. One can be exposed to the risk of some sexually transmitted diseases in men and could experience penile cancer and cervical cancer in female sex partners. Balanitis and balanoposthitis - the inflammation of the glans and the foreskin can occur. There are a plethora of risks that come along with being uncircumcised—just the same with the circumcision of the spirit. Now, let's look at the uncircumcised Philistine in I Samuel 17th chapter. Do you know the story of David and Goliath? Take some time to read if not.

What was it about David? He was just a cute boy who was the least counted among his brethren. His daddy did not even esteem what was in him? He did not really have his own... he was that dirty, stinky-smelly young chap who was doing something for somebody else. He was his father's flunky – the so-called keeper of the flock! To his brothers – he must have been known as one whose presence antagonizes without words... what does that mean? Whenever he showed up – people got on the set – he was an irritant! Read the story, and you will see.

David was that of valor in God's eye, but not in the eyes of those who knew him best, supposedly! Sound familiar? Being among those who say they know you, but who you are in God is unknown to them? They do not esteem the greatness of the Lord in your life! This is very common in families – we take each other for granted. This is just a synopsis of this story... check it out.

In the 16th chapter of the book of I Samuel, David was keeping the flock of his father. Samuel, the prophet of the Lord, was looking to anoint another king at God's Word. Samuel received instruction on where to go; whose house to go to, but not the who. Samuel did what he would do; he got the horn of oil and went to Bethlehem to Jesse's house to anoint somebody! There he found stout young men of fair countenance; in other words, they looked good! They were built (bodybuilders in our day). They had the physique of a champion; to Samuel, he had found the new king. But God, in His wisdom, established a pattern not to follow. He said, I do not look on the outside of a person; that is not what I seek. He told Samuel, I have refused Jesse's first son's stature and physique! Here comes the next son...the same result! This pattern went through all of Jesse's sons, all but one. The one that was not invited to the party. The underdog - The "ruddy" boy!

Samuel wanted to know, "Is this it?" Jesse's response was surprising, too; he just knew it was one of the soldiers in the army of Saul, but Not! Here, David is summoned to the party – last, but he arrived at the tune of "this is it!" <u>Samuel received the charge to anoint the unexpected</u>. So, he did! This story is not about the history of how he became, but rather what happened after he was.

David, the underdog, was sent by his dad to bring food to his brothers in the army on the front line. When he gets there, their envy for him manifested. They felt he came to taunt them before he ever said a word. <u>NOTE: accusations will come because of who you are anointed to be!</u> Don't' trip! However, he did ask what was going on? He was told about this Philistine who taunted the armies of the Lord for forty days and apparently was unstoppable until David came at last.

David became indignant because of the mouth of this Philistine a.k.a. Goliath, so much that he went to the king and said he would do what the army could not! Boy, was he trying to wear some big shoes? The issue – he could – because God was with him. Remember, *when God is with you, you can make it!*

Long story short – David defeated Goliath single-handedly as he prophesied. Look at the characteristics of his victory. Goliath was a giant. He was a warrior, one born to war, reared up in the environment to conquer. He was fit for this, a master of war, but God had something else in mind.

Sometimes we meet people just like Goliath. They carry themselves in a bull-dozer type of way, but like Goliath, God will defeat them, if we trust Him and let Him do it.

Goliath used all kinds of verbal tactics to intimidate David. He even called him a boy! Low blow to a man-child. That was an ego and identity thing. David was not dealing with ego as he knew his identity; he was coming in the name of the Lord, not himself. Key Point: <u>When we operate to represent God, what is being said or done will not matter at all!</u> Goliath told David what he was going to do to him. Read the scripture - you'll see! That did not move David either. He stood in the strength of the Lord his God – to victory. What am I saying…?

How many giants have we experienced in life literally? Not too many! I don't see too many of them these days, not in the flesh anyhow. Instead, I hear / tell of many, sometimes multiple giants within – all around! Hanging out, bullying, loitering, soliciting, the whole nine! Just like Goliath!

Giants – one might say they do not exist anymore; on the contrary, they are more real than what you are reading right now. Consider this.

A GIANT could be anything that is magnified in your mind! Something that is hovering over you. Something you cannot seem to overcome…it never leaves! There is a torment involved—a taunting, an oppressive, and aggressive behavior. It has the mechanics to defeat you! It looks like it would take nothing to conquer you, overpower you, annihilate you, and deem you helpless! The words from the giant of your mind to you are paralyzing

– intimidating – they seem real. But think, what happened with David? All he had was a little ole slingshot and some rocks! That was enough to defeat the Giant that others could not overcome. What is being said here?

You have giants everywhere! And just like David, you must rehearse the victories that you have already won. I hope you read the story; otherwise, you will not have a clue of what I am talking about. Giants and giant advocates will speak to you, trying to talk you right out of your victory! Just like the giant was born for the purpose of defeat – <u>what were you born for?</u> No need trying to fight timidly! Wait, I heard one say, "Do it, afraid!" Valiance will come upon you because you have a willing mind! You can do it – how so because it's uncircumcised!

What is uncircumcised? Circumcision in the bible represented the rite of passage. It was a covenant between God and Jewish males – the cutting away of the foreskin. The giants in your life are unclean; anything unclean must be done away with! God is with you to get rid of the foreskin! What is with the foreskin? The foreskin is a harness/collector of bacteria, germs, and infections! It is the process that didn't happen that can be detrimental to anyone who is intimate with you in any capacity. It can produce an inflamed circumstance; it's apparent. You must cut it off! It's best to do it in its early stages.

Like David, we all must consider our anointing. Was David strong because he was anointed? No, on the contrary, he was anointed because of the circumcision of his heart and God's choice toward him. David had no problem cutting back his error and asking God for healing. He would get himself together each time he was in error.

Our heart is a magnet for infections. We must watch, clean, and cut away the excess in our lives from across the board. **We will never be able to interact with others until we do away with our overlapping flesh**! You can do it!

"For God so loved the world, that He gave His only begotten Son, that whosoever believeth in Him should not perish, but have everlasting life." John 3:16 (KJV)

"For whosoever will save his life shall lose it; but whosoever will lose his life for My sake and the gospel's, the same shall save it." Mark 8:35 (KJV)

"Verily, Verily, I say unto you, except a corn of wheat fall into the ground and die, it abideth alone: but if it die, it bringeth forth much fruit." John 12:24 (KJV)

Die and Get It Over With

What is the meaning of this saying, "Die and get it over with?' Is it indicating a strong desire to get rid of something rather quickly: ridding the atmosphere of a nuisance or just a figure of speech?

Words can be vital to the vicissitudes of life! One's adherence to a word of instruction can propel destiny or end in tragedy, depending on the instruction. Every word is critical, and its place and need should be considered daily. Remember Spiritual Fragrances.

The title says, Die <u>and</u> get it over with. Die, to stop living, the act of giving up the ghost, yielding to the eternal realm as it calls for us. In addition to dying, make it snappy; make it quick for those who do not understand that terminology!

We used to say in Pittsburgh, "Do it with the quickness!" No hesitation - don't think about it; there is nothing to ponder, "Just do it!" Death is mandatory! That indicates quite a bit. Get it over with? There is so much that comes to mind when I say that! It states that life in your person has little meaning, little worth, minimum to no significance. In fact, that is the truth based on this text where Jesus is talking to His disciples about being born again with the hopes of prospering in God.

Death is required in life and for life. Life does not begin until death shows up and takes hold; then, life forever is initiated! These few moments as vapors on earth have absolutely no bearing on the eternal, long, forever that we face once our eyes close. Some people long to die, realizing that they will be void of earth-life trials and tribulations; that's why suicide is at an all-time high; not realizing that life after death is the real deal: you start living then! So, what is being said in this biblical concept?

Jesus told the people in John 12; His hour had come. What on earth was He talking about: His death? The purpose to which He was born, and that was to die! He came just to die so that His death could be as a seed going into the ground and germinating to bring forth the beauty of the flower's harvest. His intent was to yield, both to and through. If He had not died, He would be alone. No one would be able to receive Him and become the sons of God. But in His death brought life for the Father, which brought forth many sons, including you and me.

It is just the same when we choose to die to ourselves and to those around us; we begin to yield exponentially; rather, He yields exponentially in us. We are just a device, a receptacle that aids in the process. Maybe the shovel, the rake, the fertilizer – who knows except God. It is His choice to use us. NOTE: the rake, shovel, and fertilizer DOES NOT have a mind of their own. It does whatever the purchaser, possessor prescribes. It's dead to feelings, attitudes, and personal ambitions; it's dead to purpose until used! Its meat is to do the will of him that purchased it and finish the work – sound familiar?

God wants to use us without us in operation. He wants a "Yes." We have been "bought" with a price! A hefty cost of life has been given: a ransom for many. We are His prize possessions that He desires to show off on the earth! Manifest a harvest of Himself - to be the beauty to behold in the eye of whoever is looking. The sacrifice that considered not His own self but became obedient unto death… the death of the cross, that He might be the first born among many brethren.

We are dead (spiritually) in trespasses and sin until Christ, Who is our life, has come. He doesn't come in us until death to self comes. Once the realization that we are not living is present, we die and then are made alive in Him where we live, move, and have our being.

The base scripture in John 12:24 opens with Verily, which is to say truly or certainly. Verily is stated twice, which also means that whatever follows this is an important word to establish something significant. It is to draw your attention to a statement, a check this out approach to bring someone into the knowledge of a thing.

1. The word "Except," what does this mean? Unless something happens or takes place, the preceding will not come to fruition; it will not manifest.

2. "Corn of Wheat"- also known as a "kernel of wheat," the seed from which the wheat plant grows. The breaking forth through the outer process to begin to progress from inside to out. It is

what has been identified as wheat and not tare, the purity of the grain that grows for the purpose of provision.

3. The "fall," it is needful for us to have a dirt experience. We run or brace ourselves from it - this low-down position, not realizing this is where we experience the elevation. The bruises acquired are pivotal in life for growth and recall; they are reminders of what to do or not. The fall is an internal picture of where we came from and where we are going! Have you heard the statement, "It's only up from here!" the fall is inevitable…don't resist it…it must take place…the point is what happens after the fall. (See Adam)

   a. Who is to say that the fall of man was not the plan of God all along; since He is God, He does know what He is doing.

   b. If God led the children of Israel into the wilderness to prove what was in their hearts, would it be unlikely for the "fall of man" to be the plan in His hand?

   c. Only the pure in heart shall see God…that scripture still stands sure. Purity will allow you to see this correctly.

d. It was in the wilderness that they saw the promised land.

  e. In this life, our hearts must be in the right standing to see God; the same rules apply then and now.

  f. God is still proving us through chance and opportunity. Through trials, through circumstances, through persecutions, through peril and sword. The point is not what is going on; it is what happens next! What matters is the end result – the getting up!

4. Something has got to "Die" …it might as well be me! (not necessarily physical)

  a. When death comes, something has taken over.

  b. Death is yielded to, not resisted. Resistance doesn't matter anyhow! We are going to die some way or another; we choose. Yielded or kicking and screaming! Yes, we can refuse to die by giving up ourselves, but there are grave consequences that lead to spiritual death; being out of touch with God. Who really wants that?

  c. It is evitable. It is appointed once for man to die, and after that, the judgment.

    d. So, it is not dying that is important; it is the after effect, "the judgment," that is the concern. What shall be our end result?

    e. What good has come out of the fall if the after effect doesn't respond appropriately - to yield the desired results? What good was it to fall? *(See children of Israel in the wilderness; some had to die, or something else would have taken place)*

5. "It abideth alone…"

    a. The objective is for wheat to become something – more.

    b. Harvest to be yielded; more than one, but many.

    c. Produces others from one corn of wheat – the exponential effect.

    d. If the fall didn't come, and death of self didn't take place, production could not manifest. Death is the pathway to life.

    e. There could be no harvest of more; plenty, without the surrender to death.

    f. No chance of multiplication is possible without it.

g. If it abides alone, it never makes the connection *(see the life cycle of reproduction, the egg, and the sperm is required)*. No life ever comes forth.

h. To be by oneself is not ideal for yielding fruit (see Acts 2:42, 47)

i. Being alone manifests an Anti-Christ spirit; it is against pro-creation. Me, Myself, and I can't make it happen!

6. But if… By chance, it dies…

   a. "IF" - a word of condition

   b. Die to self

   c. Die to the world

   d. Die to things of the past

   e. Die to reacting to circumstances

   f. Die to the words of others

   g. Die to outside influences (natural and spiritual)

h. To die; deteriorating from the current state, returning to the original state, where things were productive and obedient, without option.

Get this: whether you die and go to hell or heaven, you are going to live there forever productively yielding the fruit of your life's increase; in obedience because it's without your consent at this point! It's a mandate, a summons, a must—judgement!

I. Communion with God is necessary on the regular to be considered the desired norm. (Genesis 1)

7. It bringeth forth...much fruit – now, isn't that a sight for sore eyes? Death brings forth - MUCH! This really doesn't make sense! Death is supposed to be the end of a thing, not the beginning of it! As we know it, when one ceases to exist, everything about it is at a halt; time, progress, process, growth, purpose – never to be reactivated; it's over, but not really! It has just begun!

   a. The fact that it bringeth forth says there's productivity in death.

   b. Yielding results after its own kind

   c. Walking in purpose & fulfilling its intended purpose

d. Bearing more seeds to produce more fruit in its season

e. Fulfilling the ordinance of God

f. Manifesting His workmanship

g. It becomes nourishment to others having multiple tasks and assignments

h. The end is displayed as God has so declared

It all started with Except the Corn of Wheat fall into the ground and die…

Die and get it over with…

The lack of our death is hindering a lot of things from happening on the earth. We wonder why the body of Christ is not unified; because many have fallen and could not get up. They fell, but nothing took place in addition to; the AND never showed up: therefore, it was just a fall that yielded other stuff:

- Shame
- Pride
- Embarrassment
- Reproach against God
- 7 other devils worse than the first

The word says, but if it dies, by chance, we forget who we are and take on the mind of Christ. If, by chance, we put on the whole armor of God. If, by chance, we put off the old man and put on the new man created in Christ Jesus unto good works…what would happen in us?

What would happen to others around us? What would the world be then? The connection would be made. We would become a people and not still in the singular form.

When looking at this text, it was necessary to break each word down to come to the significant truth, to understand what is being said. This was demonstrated; so, what is the summation? Can we die and get it over with, so the KINGdom can come in us and manifest His will on the earth? The benefits are endless. The beauty is inevitable – just yield and die! So, ask – God, what is still living?

Spiritual Fragrances

"*Then said Jesus unto* **His** *disciples, If any man will come after Me, let him deny himself, and* **take up his cross**, *and follow Me*". Matthew 16:24 (KJV)

"*And when He had called the people unto Him with* **His** *disciples also, He said unto them, Whosoever will come after Me, let him deny himself, and* **take up his cross**, *and follow Me.*" Mark 8:34 (KJV)

"*And He said to them all, If any man will come after Me, let him deny himself, and* **take up his cross** *daily, and follow Me.*" Luke 9:23 (KJV)

Go Limp

What does it mean to go limp? It means several things; at least, it can mean several things. When I think about going limp, I think about the body without bones or any firm substance. There is no resistance, no shape of its own, without any general direction; it seems blah!

The English definition of the word limp is an adjective. It means lacking internal strength or structure, not stiff or firm, without energy or will. Having no choice is already the opposite of man. Everything man does is determined, fashioned, thought out, deliberated, felt, desired, and often executed without thought. I just said what man does is thought out; how can they do it without thinking. It is done without second-guessing oneself, without counsel, without question, and without God.

I said that going limp meant several different things. First, it is done without resistance. It doesn't have a shape of its own. It has no known direction; it's without energy or will, no internal strength or structure. Limp gives way to its circumstance or surroundings. I had a brother many years ago. He was in a car accident; it was a significant accident. His life could have been lost, but what saved him was his inebriation. Inebriation caused his body to give way to the crash, the impact, the blow, the force that threw him out of the windshield. He lives today to tell a story that he does not remember.

Research shows that an intoxicated person is more likely to survive an automobile crash than a sober person. Why? Because the sober person braces themselves - resisting what is happening. In that resistance, the body stiffens and doesn't give way to what is taking place. Every action works against the force of the accident and its intention. In some cases, the sober driver dies or suffers life-long injuries due to their resistance. Why am I saying all of this? Because we try to brace ourselves from everything, sometimes even from good!

Man has developed a defense mechanism that works subconsciously – without thought. It is programmed into our DNA, and over time it fortifies. It happened in the Garden of Eden when Adam and Eve were deported to the earth's uttermost parts to care for themselves because of their disobedience. As a result, they gained access to the part of Gods' all-knowingness; but their access was perverted because of sin. And because man continued to operate in this perverted and distorted mindset, the propensity to protect remained.

God is ever endeavoring to get man to trust His rule, His Word, His Spirit, His Voice, His Plan… need I say more. It's not theory – it's a fact… read your bible!

Bracing ourselves preempts God – the Creator, from maneuvering the necessary that brings us to a productive place! We buck when we do not understand what is happening when we should yield. Our mechanisms are off because of our forefather's sin, which ultimately is our sin as well if we allow it to be!

If we were intoxicated with God's Spirit and allowed Him to permeate our vessels, we would experience life as we have never known. Isn't it interesting that alcohol is identified as "spirits?" We have a spirit that can operate by another Spirit/spirit; we choose which Spirit/spirit operates. Bracing happens because of the lack of trust! One doesn't trust what is happening, so the defense comes.

What exactly am I saying that can be described in this short writing? I am saying this – Stop, let us consider our ways! No defense, no fight; whatever is going to happen - let it! Trust God that He has us – that He alone can keep us during whatever by His Spirit! Sometimes life seems like one being thrown from a car, but when God is present, the impact does not and cannot have law over us without His permission. What kind of Father would He be?

One would say people die in car accidents all the time (we'll call life situations car accidents for this purpose). Indeed, they do; however, we are not privy to all aspects, scopes, or spheres of reference concerning those situations; therefore, we can't really speak to it! The news is biased, the by-standards/on-lookers biased, other parties involved – are biased too. The only non-bias is God and perhaps the person directly affected! They, too, have limited perspective as to what really happened behind the scenes. We are always trying to be God and figure out this and that! That's why He is the Creator of all things; let Him do it! We have no idea what is before us, behind us, around us, and in front of us, but He does. Go Limp – who is our defense? Flesh or God?

The scripture says, "Cursed is the man that trusts in man and makes flesh his arm." (Jeremiah 17:5a) What is He saying? Our protection, our covering is Jehovah. Man falls and cannot sustain us! He cannot maintain himself. God gave us His breath to cause life; in Him, we live, move, and have our existence – it is not in self or others.

At times, we find ourselves engaging in practices that exalt flesh above the knowledge of God, which ends in disaster. When we decide to be God instead of living as gods, independent of He who was, is, and is to come, we shipwreck! We can be very confident in the ability of the God who made the heaven and the earth… by the way, God made man for earth's purpose. How can we eliminate the manufacturer's instructions and warranty? Instructions give directions on use - the how-to; the warranty, on the other hand, is our assurance. Rest don't fight. Do not brace the blow; leave life to God; He is the Sustainer. Go limp and let it be! Relinquish the stance of defense that yields a posture of distrust. It results in barrenness and turmoil.

In the bible, you can see Jesus going limp: In the Garden. Do you think Him being flesh really wanted to continue? I beg to differ. He prayed three times the same prayer "Get me out of this!" However, Jesus, unlike His brethren, yielded to the force of what was coming for the value of the end result. (Hebrews 12:3) Going Limp is the same. When we understand the outcome, we can yield in and to the process, regardless of the experience.

In the beginning, I said, I had a brother some many years ago. He was in a car accident; it was a significant accident. His life could have been lost, but what saved him was his inebriation. Inebriation caused his body to give way to the crash, the impact, the blow, the force that threw him out of the windshield. He lives today to tell a story that he does not remember. A story that he does not remember? Yes!

When we go limp and yield to the impact of the whatever, under the unction of the Spirit of God, we can have impact without shock! We live to tell a story that we do not recollect; all we know is that God did it. He brought us through the trial, the experience that we would have otherwise been assassinated. Go Limp, and let it be, is the only reality that man faces with the inability to do it consistently! We understand that practice makes perfect. So, practice and Go Limp!

"Thus saith the LORD of hosts, I remember that which Amalek did to Israel, how he laid wait for him in the way, when he came up from Egypt. Now go and smite Amalek, and utterly destroy all that they have, and spare them, not; but slay both man and woman, infant and suckling, ox and sheep, camel and ass." I Samuel 15:2-3 (KJV)

KILL IT!

Isn't it amazing how we fear spiders, bees, rats, etc.? We are adamant about seeing the death of these things; they apparently pose a threat to us. We call pest control, rodent control, and whatever other control is required to rid us of these pests. The tenacity, the determination; there's an effort that we exert to get to the bottom of our situation. We go to all ends to gain possession of effective traps, sprays, powders, plug-ins – everything and anything to STOP the problem. We will spend countless amounts of dollars to bring the situation to a halt! It is a priority to us – something we just can't live with! It is a pressing nuisance! All of this makes sense – there is a pest in the midst. But what about when we have pests in our hearts? Hmmm, it takes another connotation, doesn't it? When it's time to look introspectively, our focus becomes clouded, and less is done to rid ourselves of the soulish pest.

In I Samuel 15, we see that God had a major issue with the Amalekites. He made it personal and charged the prophet to deliver a direct instruction for the King - slay them ALL! In the King's grandeur, he disobeyed God by saving the King of the Amalekites. As a result, the Amalekites surfaced again in David's time right after Saul. <u>What you don't kill will come back to kill you!</u>

Saul had the charge to utterly destroy the people that disturbed God and His people. God hired a pest control operator (King Saul) to rid them of those pests that constantly disturbed peace – they were a threat to the people of God. Don't you hate when you hire someone to do a thing in your home, for your event, at your church, on your job, and they do it partially? They are ineffective in their doings, and you paid them to perform it with excellence! That's disturbing to me! Saul sought to do what God had said but got turned around in the process – his GPS was off.

He surveyed the Amalekite people – the King and some unspotted animals and did not obey what God said but rather brought back into the house of God the same pest that constantly disturbed them. That sounds like someone who has rats, roaches, or any pests that they feed to breed, so they can remain.

God was angry that Saul disobeyed Him. He knew what was waiting down the road to multiply and to continue their pesty efforts because the operator failed to perform the duties assigned. This is where we are when it comes to our house – the habitation for the Spirit. We need the same tenacity to rid our spiritual home of pests as we have with our physical.

There are many pests that wander in our hearts. Pests that bite and cause sickness and disease of the spirit. Kill them all! We can't skip over it because it's us; because it's us, we can't skip over it!

Sometimes we really do not want to see what is in the house, in our house. Have you ever lived with anyone that keeps walking over the same piece of paper on the floor? Didn't they see it like you did? Well, here, you have the right to discard it. The problem: when you are dealing with someone else's spiritual house, you just can't pick it up off their floor – you don't have that kind of power, let alone influence. Only they can give you access to do it, and still, you are not doing it - God is.

We must recognize and do what it is that needs to be done. Shame is not a factor when you have pests as your mess. It's a shame not to fix it - not to kill them! Don't be a lover of nature – sinful. Kill them all!

"And He said unto me, My grace is sufficient for thee: for My strength is made perfect in weakness. Most gladly therefore will I rather glory in my infirmities, that the power of Christ may rest upon me.

Therefore I take pleasure in infirmities, in reproaches, in necessities, in persecutions, in distresses for Christ's sake: for when I am weak, then am I strong." II Cor. 12:9-10 (KJV)

Don't trip – I got this: Grace!

Grace and a pan; what are their similarities? And how is it that we become strong in weakness?

I was thinking about cake batter. Why cake batter? Because it is made up of many ingredients – many devices are used to construct this to perfection. All these ingredients have been measured, assembled in the bowl, and stirred together. They conform to each other – they become one with each other. They are no more individuals with their own identity: flour, milk, eggs, etc. They have enjoined themselves, per the maker's expectations.

What is its consistency? It's unstable - incapable of being shaped. The batter before it meets the pan is weak and fragile; it's loose in its contents and can leave traces of itself everywhere it touches, sometimes leaving a bunch of mess to clean. When we are making a cake, the batter is scraped from the bowl being poured into the pan. Our circumstances have their ways of scraping us. There is always residue left in the bowl after the batter is poured out. What's your residue? God's grace is likewise the same.

When God is through pouring us, there are contents remaining; in other words, this is the content that was excluded, and this is the stuff that cannot be used by God. Only what has gone into the pan is to be used by the Master.

The pan symbolizes Grace - God's unmerited favor, and it is His unmerited favor through faith that we are saved. It is a gift of God according to Romans 2:8, so it is the Grace of God that holds the fragile contents of our minds and our existence together. It is when we are surrounded by His grace that we gain strength, support, and confidence to become what He has purposed.

As in the making of a real cake, there are many different shapes of pans; bundt pans, sheet cake pans, round pans, and square pans. God knows just what type of cake He is creating; all we need to do is be the substance willing to be poured into whatever pan He desires.

Now, how does Grace tie together with this pan? II Corinthians 12th chapter talks about how God used Paul and had given him an abundance of revelations. Because of God's choice, Paul could have very well positioned himself in an exalted place – thinking more highly than he ought. To ensure that his feet remained on the ground, there was given to him a "thorn in the flesh" a messenger of Satan to buffet him. To buffet means to pound, or to bang, or to beat, so we know that whatever the messenger came with, it was on him – pressing him. God will allow things to come up in our lives to keep us at bay, to make sure that we understand Who is in charge.

In this text, Paul sought God three times for its removal, which brings me to my scriptures in II Corinthians 12: 9-10, which reads, *"And He said unto me, My grace is sufficient for thee: for My strength is made perfect in weakness.*

Most gladly therefore will I rather glory in my infirmities, that the power of Christ may rest upon me. Therefore, I take pleasure in infirmities, in reproaches, in necessities, in persecutions, in distresses for Christ's sake: for when I am weak, then am I strong." (KJV)

Grace was the balancer for Paul, as it is for us! Grace is man's undeserving favor, the act of love that God expresses toward us. Balancing us and bringing us from inconsistent to consistent, as well as showing that we didn't receive what we really deserved because of it! It is God's way of stabilizing us, likewise, enabling us to stand despite circumstances that come our way. If God were to allow us to experience all that we've sown, there would be no way that we would be able to stand! It would be unbearable, more than we could handle. Again, grace doesn't give us what we really deserve. His grace allows us to experience the favor of God (the generosity) - giving stability to our unstable substances. Now, let's go back to the batter going into the pan.

The contents are yet unstable! It is the pan that provides safety and strength to keep the contents from spilling all over the place. "Now unto Him, that is able to keep you from falling..." Jude 1:24. If it wasn't for God's grace, we would be everywhere; scattered brains, flighty, emotional wrecks, silly, all because our fleshly ways are unstable in comparison to God's soundness. It is His grace that provides the strength, so we do not spill over into everything and everyone in reach.

This pan gives the batter its shape; it holds it together until that time when the cake is ready to stand on its own - so to speak. Grace holds us together. God's goodness towards us enables us to stand still until that time WE can stand. Grace upholds us in the fragile times; likewise, His grace holds us even in times of strength. Grace purposes us to be what the Maker intended after being poured from the bowl. Sometimes life's circumstances cause feelings of instability, inconsistency, and fragility. But once we are poured out in the pan – Grace, God's Grace takes shape in us, advancing us to the next process.

Paul said I would most rather glory in my infirmities that the power of Christ may rest upon me. Now, what does this have to do with Grace? Well, it is our infirmities, circumstances, trials, and tribulations that define who, what and where we are in Christ. When the batter is poured into the pan, it is this process that determines how the cake will turn out. No matter what things come our way, it is God's Grace that is sufficient for us - it is enough to sustain us, enough to keep us (if we want to be kept), it is enough to carry us through whatever thorn that has come in the flesh to buffet it.

We need God's Spirit to discern what we are going through. It is His Spirit that strengthens; His power actively works on us, in us, for us, and through us. So, we should rather suffer for His sake, that the anointing of God becomes greater within us than ever before. Willing rather be talked about for His sake, that the fruit and gifts of the Spirit would operate through us. Willing rather be tried in the fire, that we come forth in the power of God because His Grace is plenty!

Just remember, in the actual cake-making process, this would be the 2nd to the last step before we become the beautiful cake the Master intended us to be. Let God's Grace be sufficient for you! There is still beauty to behold.

"Then said Jesus to those Jew which believed on Him, If ye continue in My word, then are ye My disciples indeed; [32.] *and ye shall know the truth, and the truth shall make you free." John 8:31-32 (KJV)*

You've Got to know it - Prove it - It's Relational

There is a scripture in the Bible that states, "And ye shall know the truth, and the truth shall make you free." Let's take a good look at this text.

"Then said Jesus to those Jews who believed on Him…" Wow, what an opening statement. For Jesus to speak the proceeding words, something had to be in place: belief.

Sometimes we feel like Jesus will just tell us or say something to us regardless. We eliminate the fact that a prerequisite may be required. We base that theory on our own desires; treating God like He is a Genie in a bottle; rub Him a little bit and make your wish! Nope! That's not God! He has a system in place - a standard, a rule of thumb. All we need to do is pay attention to what He is saying or doing to understand the request or condition. In this case, one had to simply be a believer. Let's go beyond that!

He said it to a specific people - a chosen people, a called-out people, a peculiar people, a nation of people that He put His name upon. They were His Signet – they were authentically chosen. They were not your average

Joe Smoe's; they were a specific people to Jesus. In other words, it's relational.

You might say, how so? Well, I'm glad you asked. Look at John 1:12, *"But as many as received Him, to them gave He power to become sons of God, even to them that believe on His name."* Power to become sons - to have sonship; isn't that relational? Of course, it is! It is the family of God implemented by Christ Jesus.

1 John 3:2 says, *"...now are we sons of God, and it doth not yet appear what we shall be; but we know that, when He shall appear, we shall be like Him; for we shall see Him as He is."* How so? Because the eyes of our understanding become enlightened when the revelation of Who He is illuminates in our spirit. When we accept the call into the beloved (Ephesians 1:6), we gain our perspective in Christ, and it then becomes relational.

He said this to the Jews - the people known to be God's choice - His prize, His bride!

Throughout the Bible, we see that God favored them, delivering them whenever they turned to Him, whenever they realized Whose, they were. God didn't hesitate to respond like one in a relationship. He had a particular spot in Himself reserved for them. Just as parents have for their children, family etc., in a particular place - it's relational and unconditional.

God was not biased or unjust. On the contrary, He loved them. He was deliberate and particular; He was and is intentional. Because of His divine providence, He reserved the right to do as the Sovereign God that He is toward them because of His Own thoughts. (Jeremiah 29:11) God is big on covenant, which is a word of relationship; it is an agreement. I hope that by now, you can see that exclusivity comes by way of relationships, and because of relationships, there are fringe benefits.

So, we see that Jesus, like His Father, was/is the same. He didn't commit Himself to those with ulterior motives, having no desire to be accepted in the beloved (John 2:23-24). The scripture denotes that they believed too! But there was something about their belief Jesus discerned that was not authentically relational: it was ulterior and situational.

What is yours?

Jesus did what He saw the Father do. In John 5:17, Jesus says, *"...My Father worketh hitherto, and I work."* What the Father commanded Jesus to speak and say, He did just that according to John 12:49. We can clearly see that Jesus was relational with the Father and that He also believed in the Father, which brings us to where we are in the text. Before we can hear what Jesus says, we must be in a position of relationship.

Howbeit, one does not understand the word of God until they have decided to be in a relationship with the Father; then, He opens their understanding to perceive as one ought, and not before. Now, sometimes God makes a choice to give some understanding to those prior to; that's what makes Him Sovereign – He can do whatever He desires when He desires, to whom He desires to do it! Their minimal and opened understanding draws them to the fountain for more drink!

Relationship sets the precedence for more; the gateway to advancement: the inheritance. One cannot receive an inheritance unknown. Some form of relationship must be established. For us to be able to hear with our hearts, we must be relational with God. The more that we are relational, the more advanced revelation ascends and descends. It becomes depth! The more we unveil to Him: the more He unveils to us! The law of reciprocity!

So, in this text, the preceding verse stated, *"...if ye continue in My Word, then are ye My disciples indeed."* Jesus indicated to the disciples that there was a prerequisite to discipleship. It wasn't just because He said so or called them to it; they had to prove it by hearing, accepting/receiving, doing, and continuing to do as He instructed. There was no such a thing as *"fly by night"* or *"Whoop, there it is!"* They had to manifest their beliefs.

Jesus said, "If" ...this is a word of prerequisite, a word of choice, decision, volition, a word of conditions. It means something must take place for the proceeding to come forth. No present, no future either. It is a seed word. Wow, I never saw that before.

Jesus didn't leave it to His disciples to figure out the specifics of His instruction. He spoke deliberate specifics concerning what He was referring to. He said, here is what it is; you hear, accept/receive, do, and continue doing My word. Oh wow, there is so much meat in this one verse! First, we must have a willingness, openness, and an obedient ear to hear. There must be a receptive heart; we can't get to accept/receive until there is a desire to be acquainted with. One cannot accept/receive something they reject! No reluctance can be present whatsoever! An "All in" attitude must be regulated. Here's the condition: this must take place before the other will!

Often, we are in those situations and miss the fact that there is a requirement that must be appropriated for the next thing to have access. When we follow the leading of the Lord, it is an open path "leading" to the next thing. It's branches that grow for the purpose of extension. It's our bridge! Obedience must be in place!

"If ye..."; meaning we, not other people, but us – you and me; we must do this! That's another thing; often, we are looking at others and not considering that He's talking to Moi et Toi *(French for You and Me)*!

If we continue - understanding that we can't stop, pause, or detour, we must be steadfast in and remain. Pausing is prohibited; we give access for deviation. It is vital to know that our focus and diligence are keys to life; without them, no conditions are implemented, let alone met! We must be persistent! We've got to know it: and to know it is to do it.

Some people brag about their information; not realizing that information unused means absolutely nothing! The implementation of a thing validates its prominence in one's life. Jesus said, "continue in," which indicated that there was an origin - a starting point. The origin was the branch to bridge to the next part. Where do we go from here? Do we stop and start? What shall we do? The question is, what will you do?

This is the part where we DECIDE Who we belong to; "...Whose side are we leaning on..." – saith the songwriter. It's the crucible - a *situation of severe trial in which different elements interact, leading to the creation of something new:* the Y in the road that demands a response. Our actions from here out depict the validity of discipleship. <u>If we belong</u>

<u>to God and love Him as we say, then we keep His commandments as He says.</u> John 14:15 (KJV) It is then that we allow the proof of relationship to manifest for all to see. There's no shame in our game! His Word: Our pleasure. We've got to know it – prove it because it is relational!

¹⁵·"But when it pleased God, Who separated me from my mother's womb, and called me by His grace, ¹⁶·to reveal His Son in me, that I might preach Him among the heathen; immediately I conferred not with flesh and blood." (Galatians 1:15-16 KJV)

Trusting that God Called You!

Why are the accolades needed, the kudos, the acceptance of man??? Have you not known? Have ye not heard that we are "accepted in the beloved?" Adopted as children in Him? (Ephesians 1:6) This is all God's doing, and it is marvelous. (Psalm 118:23)

It is so easy just to accept the truth of the gospel and live in the peace and perfectness of the word. No fight, just yield and lay hold of. Accept the promises of God, for they are in Him Yea, and Amen! (II Corinthians 1:20) They cannot be overthrown. It is your choice, which promises you to receive; that unto death or life, eat of that fruit.

If God does the calling here, what is it to figure out? John 19:30 lets us specifically know that "…it is finished!" What needed to be accomplished for reconciliation and victory had been activated. Walk in it, ACCEPT IT. You can't change it; you might as well receive it and live as He designed - for goodness' sake - enjoy it!

Why live ye in the turmoil and toils of life, when He already said what shall be? "Be of good cheer, I have overcome the world." (John 16:33) If He is Greater, what's the problem? No acceptance of—you are not in receipt of this truth—you simply do not know it! To know the truth is to have; to have, is to-do, and the to-do is because you have believed.

The banner of victory has been given: don't you see it in the Spirit? Hasn't your inner man stood up yet? Recall to your mind the hope of the Lord, for great is HIS faithfulness. (Lamentations 3:23) This is no fluke; it's real. We have been given all things that pertain to life and unto godliness. We've been made to sit in heavenly places in Christ; act like it. (II Peter 1:3) Walk tall, hold your head up: it should be up looking unto Jesus anyhow. (Hebrews 12:2) There is only one way to go: up! God is not down... He's only down to come and lift you up! Trust God did it—called you according to His purpose. You see, this is His idea: accept it!

Trust that God called you. No introductions are necessary. No doors need to be opened; He is really the Waymaker... see it, believe it, stand in it, walk in it, and know it! You have been called and accepted in the beloved. Trust it!

When You Hear the Alarm, Get Up!

It's a warning that you have something that needs to be done!

The alarm is a sound of something that has been set for a specific time that causes the body to awaken out of sleep and begin a set task.

An alarm is not randomly set, but it has been set, so that one can fulfill the purpose at hand. Let's look at the different types of Sleepers.

Let's look at…

The One who doesn't hear the alarm at all?

Whenever one is sleeping, and they fail to hear the alarm, this person is dangerous. Why are they dangerous? Well, because a deliberate warning has been set for them, and they are unable to respond to it. They totally miss it; they aren't even aware of the alarm at all. This person has warnings sounding all around him or her, but he or she is unable to respond to them. They have been captivated by the stupor of sleep. The objective to which the alarm was set, failed.

Have you ever had someone else's alarm go off, and they did not respond to it, but it woke you up from a distance? If yes, then you know just what I am talking about.

This person in the natural is the same in the spirit sleeping and has no way to awake! They are just there – living without response to life. No knowledge of what is happening in their life; it is as though they are non-existent. How about the fact that you hear what they are supposed to hear? What was meant for them awakens you instead of them from a distance. Has the preached word affected you when it was for someone else too? Your sensitivity enables you to respond in the timing alleged, but to that one – they are without recourse.

Let's look at…

The One who hears the alarm and hits the snooze button repeatedly.

This is another dangerous person. Why are they dangerous? Well, because they can respond to the alarm; they hear it; it does the job to a degree, but the condition of their internal being won't allow them to totally respond. Something in them overrides what they know is right to do, what they set in motion for themselves.

Most of the time, one who keeps hitting the snooze, ends up getting up late, rushing, trying to prepare to get out and do what it was that they set themselves to do. **They** were held captive by the sleep (themselves) they were reluctant to release. They made themselves a prisoner of sleep (self-inflicted), and **felt** they needed more time—a few extra minutes. Unfortunately, these few moments cause a ripple effect in their day; now, the rush spirit has come, and everybody around them is affected by a few moments of snoozing. Their lag in priority. Their needless care of time. This is the same as the one who doesn't hear at all and yields no positive results! *"So, whoever knows the right thing to do and fails to do it, for him it is sin."* (James 4:17 ESV)

Let's look at…

The One who hears and turns off the alarm but never gets up!

This is another dangerous candidate. He or she can hear the sound of the warning, "it is time to get up," but they are so drained and depleted that getting up is not their intention. They knew when they set the alarm that they weren't going to get up. It was how they felt when they went to sleep. Usually, the body develops a pattern. If your body is accustomed to getting up at a certain time, you will automatically arouse around that time; it is your body's internal alarm. Your body has a divine mechanism that operates this way. The same is with the adverse. If you are used to hearing the alarm and overriding the response with self-motives, likewise, your body will become more sluggish at the time that you set the alarm to awaken you. It is a deliberate attempt to sabotage purpose in life—to delay/impede progress. This person is intentional if he/she is honest.

Our mind says well, I'll set the alarm to wake me, knowing that we really are not going to get up! This is just an excuse to say, "I was so tired, the alarm went off, but I couldn't even get out of the bed." You never planned on getting out of the bed; that was your flesh devising a scheme to do what it wanted to do. If one would be honest, you have to say that the intent is not to get up because you need your rest, as you feel. You like to sleep at this time.

Some will say, this is not always true! For the most cases, it is! I've even done it myself!

There are times of the day when we are supposed to get up, and it seems that sleep is the best at that time. It's just not a natural thing; there is something behind that! What is it? (Ponder this phenomenon)

Let's look at...

The One who gets up but then goes right back to sleep!

And who is this person that does such a thing? I have done this before. Is it dangerous? Yes, it is!

One rises, goes to the bathroom, washes their face, brushes their teeth; turns around and comes right back to the bedroom, and then decides to go back to sleep after having tasted the new day - experienced the mercies granted for the purpose of the day, and is still too tired to execute what is before them. Lethargy at its best! You can't put your hand to the plow and look back (Luke 9:62 KJV). You also cannot draw back either. (Hebrews 10:39) This sleeper is found in Hebrews the 6 chapter.

The common denominator:
Now, what do all of these have in common? Lethargy and procrastination! In every scenario, there was intention present that was never actualized, or was it? You can have intention without execution. These persons had the idea, they knew exactly what to do to map out the next day, but their choice was to do something different on the inside—having a form of purpose but denying the process thereof. Sound familiar?

In some of those cases, they were pulled by circumstances not to operate in the timing that was necessary to execute what was before them. They had convinced themselves that they could do what they wanted to do! There was no remorse or governing power to check what was wrong, which is dangerous by itself when you no longer see wrong. You are barking upon reprobation – one with no existing boundaries; they are predestined to damnation because they no longer see the truth. So, what have we identified – a determined person?

Often, we'd look at something like this and call those "dead-beat" people who could care less about time. They have no regard for it. But what we missed was the fact that they were determined to operate from another perspective...just not the normal place. They overrode what was right, defied the order, and maneuvered in their own space. We should look at this; take the good with the bad. All that is needed here is to redirect attitude toward purpose.

Time is of the essence! Our time is limited! Is there really time to lose? I do not think so because we are not the governor of the time that has been given us; that's

God's department. Our times are in His hand, according to Psalm 31:15. So, how can we afford to be any of those sleepers? One would have to determine which sleeper they are and see the impact of patterns that plays an avid role in life.

You can look at yourself; what are the ramifications that relate to you?

We can't continue knowing that we have something to do for the Kingdom, but never get around to it, because we are lackadaisical – jumping in and out of purpose from one day to another. On point one day and off the next day. Neither can we dress for the wedding and then go back to sleep because we feel the time has been delayed. The problem is that we don't know when our time is going to come full circle. It would be horrible to be lost for eternity because of sleeping on the job. We should not want anyone else performing the task that we have been assigned to do, because we can't hear the assignment. It's time to get up!

Time is not ours; God created it for us to be governed by it, and dare we squander it! So now, what are you going to do with the time you have?

Get the priorities straight! Get the mind right! Don't defy what has been established to help! Check the nonchalant behavior, and trash it. You can't afford not to… because time is of the essence, so get up! Be the sleeper that heard the alarm, arose as proposed, started the course of productivity, and nailed it! You can do it!

"And the earth was without form, and void; and darkness was upon the face of the deep." Genesis 1:2a (KJV)

"And God said, Let there be light: and there was light." (Genesis 1:3 KJV)

Look Around and Consider

His Hand Is… You've got to know – it's a Mess for a Reason.

Why did you say such a thing? Often, life is misconstrued. The essence of existence forgotten; the fullness of His plan to prosper man started out of nothing. The same nothing that was once something, that became nothing for the sake of becoming something, that He might take that nothing and make something out of it again!

In Ezekiel 37:1, it reads, "the hand of the Lord was upon me, and carried me in the spirit of the Lord, and sat me down in the midst of a valley which was full of bones…"

Let's hyper-speed this; the reason God brought Ezekiel to the place of nothing was that He was going to make it something again! It was referenced that it was an army; was it metaphoric or literal, I don't know, but He showed him present-tense, past-tense, and future-tense in one view, which is much like He does for us.

There was a matter of process required to see and accept the plan of God, in which Ezekiel was directly involved. He could not fast-forward to the next step without completing the current step like sometimes we attempt, but he had to take note of what God was doing and how He was doing it! That is another lesson you can read for yourself and get an understanding of.

Words were required to bring about a change in that geographical, environmental, and atmospheric dilemma. There was nothing but death and decay all around – no words had yet been spoken. Isn't that just like God, repeating Himself from the beginning? If you can't glean anything else from this scripture, you can glean from the words, the hand of the Lord is upon me! You must first acknowledge that the hand of the Lord is upon you in order to do what He assigns.

You must be able to see and accept that, yes, it is possible for the hand of the Lord to be upon you - despite you, regardless of you, beyond you, outside of you, and not because of you; it is the Lord's doing.

1. It means that His hand being upon you has nothing to do with what you say sometimes, "you are not," or what people sometimes say that you are. Because you are what you are by the grace of God, it is His words that fragrant your life. (I Corinthians 15:10 KJV)

2. It means that God has established your identity in Him, as He became sin that we might be the righteousness of God in Jesus Christ. Your life as you

see it doesn't make that much of a difference. If He wants to make something from nothing – you just gave Him something to work with, isn't that wonderful? (II Corinthians 5:21 KJV)

3. It means that far above what Satan whispers in your ear about what you have done, God's hand is still upon you. Because you have confessed your sin, and He is faithful and just to forgive you of your sin and cleanse you from all unrighteousness, which puts you back into right standing with Him. He became sin for us. (I John 1:9 & II Corinthians 5:21 KJV)

4. It means that man cannot reverse what God has ordained and said about you. What God has blessed; they are commanded to bless because the blessing of the Lord cannot be reversed. It's geographical, environmental, and atmospheric – the plan of God is already out there! (Numbers 23:20 KJV)

5. It means that whatever you do for Him, it's not really you who is doing it, but the hand of the Lord is manifesting His presence. Because the Father is in you, and you in the Father, it is He that is doing the work and will perform it. (John 14:10 KJV)

6. It means that you can do all things through Christ, which strengthens you, because His hand is upon

you. How it looks or has been, is no longer a factor. (Philippians 4:13)

To know that the Lord's hand is upon you is to know so much! Regardless of the mess, it is to know that it's like that for a reason and the reason doesn't matter! It is much like the certainty of knowing your name. No one can tell you otherwise. You can't be convinced that your name is not what it is. You can't be convinced of who you belong to and who your siblings are. There are some things that has been established in your family. There are just things that you can be confident in the outcome.

Coming up culturally, we knew that if a fight broke out, our sibling(s) were going to show up to make sure the fight was fair. No one else was going to get involved, if they were present. That was our confidence. They would do just what you believed and expected them to do like clockwork. So it is with the Lord. If God can give you that kind of tenacity in the natural, how much more will He do it in the Spirit!

You've got to know that His hand is upon you, regardless. You've got to know it like you know your name. You don't stand in the mirror every morning and say my name is Jane Doe, or my name is John Doe! But when it comes to the things of God, you act as if you need to get in the mirror every day and rehearse it over and over and over again. Well, if that is the case, you'd better get to it until it becomes who you are for real—until you know it like you know your name. Until it is deep down in your spirit, until it is uncontestable, and you are unmovable. Until you do what you must do, because you have accepted the Lord's hand upon you. You must know that His Spirit is upon you and with you.

Now, did you read it thoroughly? It also said, "… And carried me out in the spirit of the Lord," Now what is this here? The Spirit of the Lord picks someone up and takes them somewhere – to a place of death, where no life is?! He is governing our will according to His! You can't go anywhere in the flesh! The Spirit is what fosters the atmosphere for movement. He controls what happens, where you go – not you! So, where did He carry him (Ezekiel) out of? Out of himself? Hmm!

Ezekiel had to be <u>transported out of himself to a place in the spirit where he could see God.</u> How was this possible? It was the ease of seeing God where there was no life except for God! He wants us in that place where our focus is on Him as the Way, Truth, and the Life, and in order to do this, sometimes there must be death!

The text then says he was carried and **sat** down in the midst of the valley. In the midst of; right-smack and dead center! He could not go past! He could not escape. He was not on the scenic route or the shortcut; he was front and center. What does the valley represent? Does it mean that it is a resting place, a place of relaxation, and a place where you plan to be for a while.

When you sit, it is indicated that you are in relaxation mode—relaxing in the Valley? This has always been associated with something dormant or mundane, never relaxation. The valley has always been known as hardship; in the place where nothing is coming together – where lack is…what's different here: God!

Sometimes God must carry you to a place where there is nothing all around you because you will find something to depend on – put your hope in! Someplace where there is no life or no hope; then, He lays the *"whammy"* on you – the mystery of His will in your vulnerability. Can you handle the knowledge? What are you going to do about it? It just didn't stop there; it was the valley where bones were! This is getting better and better. You're in a valley full of bones, full of death – seemingly, nothingness!

Bones once was, but now aren't. But God wanted to take the something that became nothing for the sake of becoming something again from the nothing that it became, in order to manifest something out of the nothing it had become! This is what is forgotten, and it's this: if God's hand is upon you, it doesn't matter what happens, where you are, what people do or say, how raggedy the situation becomes; how hopeless/helpless it appears – He is your Help/Hope! You must acknowledge that sometimes His will houses hardship for proving purposes – God wants bragging rights. Remember Job? Can He say the same about you?

You have got to know that you have been equipped with everything needed to do it! To do what? Whatever God says for you to do! Don't judge it; just do it! What has He said?

Remember, it was impossible for those bones to live in Ezekiel's day without the Word of God. Some things are impossible right now, but not with God! (Luke 1:37) Trust His purpose for you and know that His hand has selected you! It is like this for a reason! God is not void of understanding knowledge – He knows, and He sees it all!

Now, the question is not, Lord, what is the reason? But rather, the answer is Yes, Lord!

"Thy Word have I hid in mine heart, that I might not sin against Thee." Psalms 119:11 (KJV)

"The entrance of Thy word giveth light; it giveth understanding unto the simple." Psalm 119:130 (KJV)

"Thy word is a lamp unto my feet, And a light unto my path." Psalm 119:105 (KJV)

Even in the Darkest Situation, There Is Light.

Amid whatever we are going through, there is always light. In the earth, we call the Night a period of darkness, yet it is never totally dark. The moon powers the earth. There are lights on the houses, on the streets, which illuminate in darkness; some are powered by the Sun (all puns intended). If God made it so that there is not total darkness on the earth, why would He let total darkness reign in our lives? That contradicts the God of order and His actions. He is strategic and does things on purpose. He is a God of Purpose. He never does anything haphazardly.

So, if God allowed light to be and allowed us to create more methods of potential light—enabled to illuminate in complete darkness, we can rest assured that in our situations, circumstances, there is a light that He has also provided. That light is what He has allowed us to generate ourselves by His Spirit. So, where is the light?

We know the moon to be the light that shines in the Night. Although, it doesn't shine like the sun, yet, it does shine bright enough to illuminate the sky. Since all truth is parallel, we then should recognize the moon's kind-of light in our situations and its purpose.

Often, we look for the Sun to shine all the time in our lives, forgetting that if God made the Night and Day, the chances are that we will experience the same in our lives. He created nighttime to be a time of rest. The night is supposed to be our resting time. The day is when we work. Do you hear what is being said here? We have this mixed up! The Night is for rest, and the Day is for work!

The day is, in our lives, the time when you seek the Lord while He may be found; to call upon Him while He is near…this is our time to pursue God like never before. In most cases, the day is not the prime time for seeking Him. We want to pursue God when there is a problem in our midst. We are in relax mode during the day and panic mode at night. But remember, Night is to be the period of rest…what does this mean, not to pursue God? On the contrary, it is simply the time of rest – to lay your burdens done, to have the expectation for morning coming. Not the time of staying up worrying about it! It's not the time to miss sleep trying to figure it out! The day was made for that; <u>provisions need to have already been made for the night season coming.</u> The word says, "…work…while it is day: the night cometh when no man can work." (John 9:4) It is working in the day of our situations so that when night comes, we can rest!

Now there are those instances in our lives that major work happens at night, for example, "road workers." Their aim is to prepare the way for us! But notice just how much light they create so that they can effectively work. Where is our light? Regardless of the work environment, we've got to have the light within us shining brightly. "Let your light so shine before men, that they may see your good works and glorify your Father which is in Heaven." (Matthew 5:16 KJV) *Shining is not an option but a mandate.* Lord help me!

On one of my live sessions of ImprompTWO with my husband, I talked about when we purposely turn the light off ourselves because of what we purposed to do in our hearts to satisfy our flesh. The scripture says, "Let your light…", which indicates that we can preempt the illumination. Not only do we hinder ourselves, but we hinder other people, in which we shall give an account. For those that have experienced "Oaties" – roaches or any kind of bugs for that matter, when you turn the light on, they scatter. Why? Because they cannot continue to operate where you can dispose of them, it's always in darkness. Keep that light on in you!

The scripture hath said, "Be still and know that He is God!" It is in the night season of our lives that we come to see the handy work of God. Why do we have this backward - rest in the day and work at night? Some of us just work 24/7. There is a period of time in the day that God designated for rest; our night season is that time.

Have you ever noticed that if you have a cold or something, it is at its worst at night? Why is this? Because this is a time, a period of rest…your body is responsible for replenishing itself at night. When rest doesn't take place, we are ineffective internally.

Consider II Corinthians 12:9, when God tells Paul His strength was made perfect in weakness. When the dark comes, God's strength activates and is perfected; it is His daytime. This is the time for the light of God to shine on our situations. Given that we say we have Him on the inside, then we should always have **The L.I.G. H. T.!** [The Lord - Inside - Giving - His -Thoughts] His words, His views, His decision on any matter.

As Himself, God has given us a significant amount of responsibility for what we think. He said in Proverbs 23:7, "For as he thinketh in his heart, so is he...." He told us in Romans that we have the mind of Christ; in Philippians 2: 5, He says, "Let this mind be in you which was also in Christ Jesus..." In the 4th chapter, He tells us to think about these things, truth, honesty, justice, purity, loveliness, and good report; if there be any virtue or praise, think about these things. We can say with assurance that we have the responsibility to uphold the contents of our thoughts.

II Corinthians 10:5 says, *"Casting down every imagination, and every high thing that exalts itself against the Knowledge of God..."* We are to bring into captivity every thought to the obedience of Christ. We have a responsibility to The L.I.G.H.T. in our hearts, The Lord Inside Giving His Thoughts; it should be in our hearts so much that when darkness comes, we are reminded of His thoughts - His words.

We are to do what He does, according to His word. This is why His word has to be a L.A.M.P. (Lighting - Always – My- Path). Without something to manifest through, there is nothing. The moon is in something; it's #1 in a form; #2 is in the sky. Light is in the lamp, ceiling, or whatever in our homes, but something holds it. There's not just a light bulb suspending in mid-air...something is holding it. In front of our homes, there is a lamp post on the porch, in the front yard, wherever it is; nonetheless, there is a light somewhere, and something is holding it – supporting it! Whether that something is glass or metal, it is there to protect the light from the elements that can put it out! Protection from the elements that potentially can cause the ability of the light to faulter. External things should not affect what's on the inside – remember, it is protected.

God has given us His Spirit and His Word as a security from the elements so that we may shine for all to see! Take your place on the candlestick because, in every situation, there should be light. *"...God said, Let there be light: and there was..."* (Genesis 1:3) So, where is yours?

Help Someone Else Get to Jesus. There's more than enough of Him to Go Around

A Narrative on Mark 2:1-5

1. "And again He entered into Capernaum after some days; and it was noised that He was in the house.

2. And straightway many were gathered, insomuch that there was no room to receive them, no, not so much as about the door; and He preached the word unto them.

3. And they come unto Him, bringing one sick of the palsy, which was borne of four.

4. And when they could not come nigh unto Him for the press, they uncovered the roof where He was: and when they had broken it up, they let down the bed wherein the sick of the palsy lay.

> 5. When Jesus saw **their** faith, He said unto the sick of palsy, "Son, thy sins be forgiven thee."

There are Jesus seekers. There are people who want to be where He is. People gravitate to where the Spirit of the Lord is present. The word says in 2 Corinthians 3:13, "…where the Spirit of the Lord is, there is liberty." There are many people who desire to be free. Some pay numerous amounts of money to buy something that they think will release them from life's hardships, only to find that what money can buy is not what they are really looking for - in hopes to gain the peace & freedom that they've spent out searching. Likewise, there are those who desire to be in the presence of Jesus/God that they will take whatever measures deemed necessary to get into His presence.

In this story, the people of Capernaum got word that Jesus was there at a certain house, and there was a press to get to Him. They were packing in so much that there was no more room to get into His presence. You know the feeling of how when you just feel pressed beyond measure, and you're under the attack of the enemy, there are sometimes when you can't get to Him through the door, you must go through the roof… and just scream out His name JESUS, that's all you can say is His name! Isn't it good to know that it doesn't matter how many people are in His presence; there is always room for YOU! Well, these men experienced that press, the press to get this man sick of palsy in to see Jesus.

The paralytic was stricken to the degree that he could not get up and move about like we would, had he been able. This man was restricted in his activities and limited in what he could do. But these men, the Bible indicated, came unto Him, meaning Jesus, bringing one sick of the palsy; so, they were carrying this man.

Now, I knew a little boy whose development was delayed. It took some time for him to walk on his own. Carrying him around was hard, so I can only imagine what it would be like to carry a man who could not move his body: it was like a Dead Weight, which is heavier than a normal person. They carried this man to Jesus.

There are people we encounter that we feel are a burden to us. They seem like they just can't get it together. They are tripping over their own shoestrings and everything else in their path. Every time you talk to them, they are basking in their past or in their dreary present, unable to see their future in God even when pointed out to them. Those are the ones like the paralytic that need to be carried along until they get to Jesus. Don't get weary in welldoing. I'm sure you know a few people just like this.

Now the word says, "When they could not come nigh..." meaning they had obviously repeatedly tried to come in the house by way of the door, perhaps even by way of the window, then they got this bright idea! The Bible says they uncovered the roof! Now, once again, these men are lugging this heavy man along, trying to get in through doors & windows to no avail; so, they decided let's go through the roof. What sense does this make? He is heavy on the ground! Isn't he going to be heavier in the air – I'm just saying!

Again, they had to lift this man up over people, over their own heads, to get him high enough to the roof. Certainly, I'm sure they had help from others, and I am sure there were some of us standing around on the side saying, "Huh, how stupid is that? It's too many people here; they are not going to get in! And besides, get in the back of the line anyway; I was here first! Hey, that's gypping!" All of the obstacles had presented themselves, I'm certain - it wasn't going to be easy, and I'm sure the question arose in their minds, is this worth it! All of this just to get somebody else in!?

These men were intercessors in their own right! They were more concerned about someone else rather than themselves. They had to think about how it would be if they were in his shoes. They had to think about how they would want someone to do the same exact thing for them: therefore, *they pressed!*

These men were determined to get this man to Jesus, where his healing could begin. Sometimes we see people struggling spiritually, and we do nothing but stand on the sideline and ridicule, critique, and pass judgment. For goodness' sake, they're struggling! We must become intercessors for those who are struggling. Some don't even know that they need God, so we must help them understand what it is and who they are seeking.

Sometimes people just need encouraging words, expressions of genuine concern, and of course, prayers of intercession. God never said for us to ignore each other and/or just be concerned about our own lives. But His Word in Romans 15: 1 says, "We then that are strong ought to bear the infirmities of the weak, and not to please ourselves." 1 Corinthians 8:13 says, "Wherefore, if meat make my brother to offend, I will eat no flesh while the world standeth, lest I make my brother to offend." This signifies that we should be concerned about each other and realize that the world does not revolve around us and ours. For us to walk this way of the cross, like Jesus, we need to remember it is going to have to be about someone else.

We can't just be determined for ourselves, but we need to be determined to see others healed, delivered, and made free. We are so bound by our own stuff that we can't help anybody else get to Jesus. And that's just the way Satan wants to keep it! He wants us to so be distracted by our own devils that we can't help someone else be free of theirs. If we would just stand in the gap for somebody else, God would tend to our needs.

These men's faith drew Jesus' attention! How many times do we do whatever we have to do to get someone to God? "Hardly Ever?!" We are so self-centered and think we are self-efficient; when really, we are only self-righteous. We have lost compassion for others. We have lost the desire to see others get to Jesus. Blinded by the fact that they may get something from Him that we don't have. We are simply selfish! Notice the word self in the word selfish.

Now the Bible did not indicate that these men were related to the man sick of the palsy; you know where I'm going! We will make intercession for our families, our friends, but what about someone else? These men were determined to get him into a place where he could be free. They took their time, they took their effort, they took their strength, and they took their own determination to get him to that place where Jesus was. When was the last time we'd done that?

For this man to be able to get where he was going without these men giving up, there had to be some sort of relational agreement. The Bible didn't indicate that these men knew the man or each other, but obviously, they had some type of encounter with the man to display such persistence.

Now whether the man paid them or made some type of agreement for them to get him, to the healing location, by any means necessary, they sure were determined. Why didn't they get discouraged?

Now, verse 4 of it says, ..." when they had broken it up," meaning it took more than one hammering, more than one kick or stomp, more than one tussle, it took time and strength to break up this roof. Sometimes it takes time to break up the fallow ground in us. Why did they do this for this man?

See, in those days, they esteemed the association of each other. Nowadays, we can't even stand to be in the presence of each other. We half speak, and we have got everything to say about what's wrong with everybody. But these people would take care and look after each other, and not only is this careless behavior prominent culturally, but it is also among the people of God. We could care less about the next person if they don't associate with us. And don't have your own mind or opinions and ideas about something; you are really not liked! But these people cared about their associations so that they would help this man sick with the palsy get before Jehovah Rapha, their Healer.

The Bible said that when Jesus saw <u>their</u> faith, not when He saw the sick man's faith, their determination, and the belief in knowing that Jesus was able to heal this man. I believe they were saying, "if they could but just get him before the Savior." Jesus spoke to the man that lay sick, "Son, thy sins be forgiven thee." (Mark 2:5) That was not based on the man's own plea for forgiveness; it was based on the faith of the ones making the intercession for him. The press is necessary for not just us but for the next person as well. It is when we lose sight of our own dilemma and begin to pray to make intercession for someone else to get through his or her situation, that is when our situation takes a turn for the better.

What kind of God would He be if He allowed us to pray or help others and see the fruit of our labor, and our stuff is Still in shambles—discombobulated? Now, that doesn't mean that just because we prayed, our stuff is going to turn around instantly; what it does mean is that we will begin to see something happening on your behalf, even if it is a perspective change on our part; that's change.

This knowledge should make you want to go out and start helping and praying for others more frequently so that our overwhelming little stuff can be dealt with. We know that Jesus can handle our problem, somebody else's problem, and the next person's problem too!

When we become unselfish in getting someone else to God, that is when we really begin to move closer to Him, and He begins to work things out in our lives that we did not formally petition Him for. It's just like someone doing something for us that we didn't expect, nor did we ask them to do it. And it just so happened to be that thing that we really needed. Now, we are so happy, shocked, excited, and it just makes us feel so good to the point that we are in tears because our heart is touched by the act of kindness and the meeting of a need that we hadn't publicly made known - that's God again!

And those are the types of things that He does for us when we are unselfish. When we pour out of ourselves into another, He pours Himself into us beyond our imagination. **We must help someone get to Jesus. There's plenty of Him to go around!**

What Are You Talkin'?

*I*n order to understand this reading, you have got to read Genesis 11:1-9. There are relevant - key principles that these people from the east clearly understood that we, the people of God, yet struggle with. Remember the wise men of the east?

In the opening statement of Genesis Chapter 11, beginning at verse 1, it says: **"AND THE WHOLE EARTH,** (which means nobody was left out, there were no stragglers, no late bloomers, no procrastinators, but everybody together,) **WAS OF ONE LANGUAGE, AND OF ONE SPEECH."** The power of agreement in communication.

Now, I asked myself the question, what is the difference between language and speech? Language is identified first in the text…" And the whole earth was of one *language* and of one speech." The Bible is systematic and strategic, so if *language* is mentioned first, then there must be a reason. As I researched the meanings of each word, the difference became clear.

LANGUAGE – is a dialectic or native tongue that one uses to communicate with another. It is human speech, *speech peculiar to a nation, to a people.*

In other words, by what and how I am speaking, I am known. Hispanics speak Spanish, Germans speak German, and Americans are supposed to speak English, but that doesn't always happen. Do you get the point? I am known how I talk. I can be identified by how I communicate. And what is speech?

SPEECH – on the other hand, is the faculty (capability) of speaking. In other words, speech is just the ability to produce a sound verbally with the mouth that one's ear can hear.

People can have speech without being clearly understood, and you have to keep asking them, "What did you say - What did you say?" But just because you couldn't understand them does not mean they didn't have speech. The fact that they could produce a sound from their mouth says the ability was present.

James Brown pinned a song, "Talking Loud and Saying Nothing," which simply means that I hear something, but it is not the language that I understand or speak. Speech is the functionality of communicating. So, do we understand the difference between language and speech? That's the question.

Language is how I can be identified as a people; it is what I'm accustomed to. It's who I am! *Speech* is just the ability to verbalize. *And you need both Language and Speech to be effective!*

We know that the whole earth was identified as being with one accord in their communication. Verse 2 says, **"AND IT CAME TO PASS,** (it happened, it took place, it manifested) **AS THEY** (those together, those assembled) **JOURNEYED** (as they went, as they were going, as they moved out) **FROM THE EAST,** (from, clearly indicates that the East was where they were; it was where they once were; where they had been for a while) **THAT THEY** (meaning all of them, together) **FOUND A PLAIN IN THE LAND OF SHINAR;..."**

There are 3 points in this part of the scripture:

"...They found..."

Well, in order to find, you must have been in search of; it must have been something that was lost or misplaced; something that was lacking with the knowledge that if they looked for it, they would find it.

So, in this case, they found a plain in the land.

When I think of the word PLAIN, it reminds me of something stripped-down, simple, basic, easy, without hardship, something pure. Something without A fight! No ups, no downs; no ins, no outs; no mountains, no valleys; no hills to climb; a flat place where everything could be seen without surprises! They found simplicity in the land.

And what is Land – it is the ground, earth, territory. It is an asset, a possession, and its equity. It's something of value. So, they were in search of something of value without the fight - simplicity. Isn't that what the people of God would like to have, **SOMETHING OF VALUE WITHOUT THE FIGHT** - wells they didn't dig, houses they didn't build, vineyards and trees they didn't plant? Well, these people found this in a plain, in the land of Shinar.

It is important to give the place where you are a name. Just as Isaac did when he was digging the wells in the days of his father Abraham, in the 26th chapter of Genesis. The people of the land strove; they contested for each well he dug. And he gave each place a name because it was symbolic, it was a reminder - it stood for something! Give the place where you are going a name too!

So, when they found this place, the scripture says, "...**AND THEY** (all of them, together again) **DWELT THERE.**" (They hung out a while; they stayed; they set up camp in this place; they made it home - together).

Verse 3 says, "**AND THEY SAID ONE TO ANOTHER**, (Okay, here is the language and speech thing again. For one to say to another; for me to say to you, and you say to me, we <u>must</u> first have the ability to speak. And <u>then</u>, be willing to open our mouths and do it. Speaking in such a way that we understand each other. We must be unified before we open our mouths – having all things common because we are known by that tongue. So, what are we talkin'?)

THEY SAID ONE TO ANOTHER, GO TO..." (This is key – "...**Go...**" - is an action; it requires a response in position – it's movement. "...**To...**" - is a direction; it points out specifics. When they spoke one to another, they reciprocated an action with direction. Often, we speak, but we don't have the action or direction; it's just rhetoric! It's just words!

But they said, in addition to, go to, "...**LET US** (meaning everybody, all together, being with one accord, having the same mind one with another, unified with purpose) **MAKE BRICK...**" Understand that the making of brick was not their ultimate reason for traveling, but brick would become the main source needed to produce the vision. What is it that we need to produce the vision in our lives – has it been identified? Brick would become the foundation of the matter. Now we understand that they obviously had a vision that took preparation to bring it to fruition. Let's go on… they said, *"…let us make brick* **AND** (in addition to, the scripture says) **THEY BURNED THEM THOROUGHLY…"**

So, not only did these people understand that the greater purpose would need a foundation, but they understood that it would need to be strong and tried. How is it that we, the people of God, don't and won't understand that we are going to be tested? *I Corinthians 3:13 says, "Every man's work shall be made manifest: for the day shall declare it, because it shall be revealed by fire; and the fire shall try every man's work of what sort it is."* How is it that the world knows that we've got to test stuff out!? When they make a new model car, they use "Crash Dummies" to test out its impact and safety. Whenever they bring a new product on the market, they test it on animals—not saying this is right, but there is the concept of testing involved. If the world understands this principle and knows not God, why then don't we understand His language? What are we talkin'? The scripture says, **"AND THEY HAD BRICK FOR STONE, AND SLIME HAD THEY FOR MORTER."** It didn't say that they made slime; it states that they made brick: the strong part of the equation. Slime was used to hold the bricks all together – it was for cohesion. The scripture said they had slime for mortar to keep it all together. What you need to make what you're doing stick - to make it all work together, you've already got! Verse 4 says, **"AND THEY SAID**, (all of them; togetherness again) **LET US** (that's everybody) **BUILD US A CITY, AND A TOWER..."** Now we are getting to the nitty-gritty!

The vision was to build. In order to build a city, one must first have a people who would occupy the city. So, the people needed to be built up before the city could be built. (This is critical in any ministry) The preparation was to make brick using what they already had to make it work together. But first, they had to move from where they were; to the simple place of value that they sought out and named. Not only that, but to speak the same things and be identified by what they spoke. Not only were they going to build a city but a tower as well. They had the mindset; that if we are going to do this, then we might as well do that too, while we are at it! They said, **"GO TO, LET US BUILD A CITY AND A TOWER, WHOSE TOP MAY REACH HEAVEN..."** This tower was to be built that its top reaches unto heaven. They wanted to reach Heaven – Heaven? Here is my imagination about how they were thinking. While we are building up a people, we might as well compile all our knowledge; might and strength, resources, finances, and everything that we've acquired, until what we have is great! Until God responds! They had the right concept with the wrong intent!

They said, **"...AND LET US MAKE US A NAME..."** Sometimes we have this idea to make a name for ourselves instead of lifting the name of Jesus. Instead of Him being glorified and exalted, we exalt ourselves and people. Our intentions, as *"His people, the sheep of His pastures,"* should be to lift Jesus up and make His name Great on the earth. Did they want a reputation, prestige, accolades, recognition: but for what - self-gratification, to be seen; for approval of others, to be men-pleasers? I don't know; maybe for the same reason why we steal God's Glory! They went on to say, **"...LEST WE BE SCATTERED ABROAD UPON THE FACE OF THE WHOLE EARTH."** Oh, they had big plans, to be known all over the world! They, like some of us, had their own agenda. This name was to be so that they would not become scattered upon the face of the earth, but to become identified, distinguished, centered out, set apart, called out! The problem with them, they did not understand that their being of one language and of one speech was enough identification. God distinctively desired the same thing for them, to be the Ecclesia – His body. They were seeing yet blind, hearing yet deaf. Speaking, but "ain't" saying nothing. What were they talkin'?

Yes, they went down in history, written in the Bible for men of all races, color, national origins, and creeds to read. What they did not understand was the very fact that they moved from the place where they were and sought out a better place with a name and abode in it. They prepared a strong foundation and allowed it to be thoroughly tried; they spoke and rehearsed one to another the vision, in the process of building up a people, and compiled all the knowledge and resources available would be plenty to make their name great! As a matter of fact, God was watching! Not because they were building a city or a tower, but because they were of one language and speech!

Look at verse 5, it says, **"AND THE LORD CAME DOWN TO SEE THE CITY AND THE TOWER, WHICH THE CHILDREN OF MEN BUILDED."** (Not the children of the Lord, but the children of men; so, they were of the world. Now how is it that the people of the world know how to get the attention of our God sometimes faster than we?) Something to think about!

"**AND THE LORD SAID,** (Well-well-well, the children of men's unity prompted the Lord to speak and say) **BEHOLD, THE PEOPLE IS ONE, AND THEY HAVE ALL <u>ONE LANGUAGE</u>; AND THIS THEY BEGIN TO DO:** (what was He referring to, "…and this they begin to do…" One would say it was the tower, but I believe it was the unity of language and speech – it had never been done before! Else there would have been another account when God came down to see. Unity is the commanded blessing.) **AND <u>NOTHING WILL BE RESTRAINED FROM THEM, WHICH THEY HAVE IMAGINED TO DO</u>."** Nothing restrained…? That is a blank check to see the manifestation of God's creation.

What would God do if we, His people, would be of one language - His language, and go with the vision, moving from where we are, in search of something better, that **we** can name. Preparing what is necessary, using what we already have, speaking strong, and rehearsing it one with another—putting our hands to the plough and fulfilling His plan, so that it might touch heaven. Making a name for the Lord, and the whole earth know it! What would it do for the Lord?

Matthew 5:16 says, *"Let your light so shine before men that they may see YOUR good works and glorify your Father which is in Heaven."* What if we stuck together as a people of God? He would be obligated to show up and show out; to do something that has never been done before, making His mark on the Earth; going down in History. If we would speak the same thing, and not just make noise, and do something that would uplift the vision, not tear it down, God would come and see about what we are doing. But it's all in what we're talkin'; what we're confessing. What saith us of the matter? What do we think in our hearts? What are we talkin'? Let's bring this to now.

Do we *edify* the vision of the house, or do we *nullify* it? Do we *initiate* action towards the vision, or do we *cause regression*? What we say is what we are known by. We must come together as a people: to build what thus saith the Lord and speak His word only. If language identifies a peculiar group of people, then what is our problem?

I Peter 2:9-10 says, "But ye are a chosen generation, a royal priesthood, an holy nation, a peculiar people; that ye should shew forth the praises of Him who hath called you out of darkness into His marvelous light:" We should stand out to the world. There is an old song I used to sing as a child, "Everybody ought to know, everybody ought to know, everybody ought to know, Who Jesus is." They should know who we are and Whose we are. Bill Gates and Donald Trump should not be the big wigs on the scene, meaning the world should not use them as the patterns to follow, but men should know the people of God *as His people* to follow.

Verse 10 says, "Which in times past were not a people but are now the people of God: which had not obtained mercy, but now have obtained mercy." He has changed who we were;

He has engrafted us into the beloved. We are to speak His language and be known by that!

II Corinthians 5:17-19 says, *"Therefore, if any man be in Christ, he is a new creature: old things are passed away; behold, all things are become new."*

[18] And all things are of God who hath reconciled us to Himself by Jesus Christ, and hath given to us the ministry of reconciliation: [19] To wit, that God was in Christ, reconciling the world unto Himself, not imputing their trespasses unto them, and hath committed unto us the <u>word</u> of reconciliation." And hath committed unto us the word (what one speaks) of reconciliation. Surely, if the wicked can get results, so can we.

If the wicked can get God's attention, then so can we…for *"we are His people, the sheep of His pasture."* He is concerned about what we're doing, and He is concerned about what we are speaking. So, ask yourself the question. **"What Am I talkin'?"** We are to line our words with the Word of the Father and build.

With God, There Is No Guesswork

There are many things in life that are uncertain, having many variables, and becoming unpredictable. From day to day, our environment as we know it mutates into something that we have never seen before.

With the pandemic taking our world by storm, ending many lives, and for some, life has just begun. All these changing components have a great part in man determining his own way, trying to create what he feels is stability when he is sinking in quicksand. Quicksand? They tell me that with quicksand, the more you try to get out of it, the more you become deeply embedded for a sure drown in this thick tar-like substance that exists or does not exist – humor me with the subject, as we know it to be.

We are always attempting to wiggle our way out, not knowing that He is solidifying fate even more. Man is always adding his spin on the things he feels he has authority to govern. This is why it is so important to have God-fearing folks in positions of power, but that's another story to tell!

What is being said here? Everything that is done where man is concerned vacillates, shifts, morphs into something else more devastating than its previous version, becoming easier to be consumed in! We find that what was a "no-no" in the day our parents, grandparents, and great-grandparents is now the standard with a new twist—accepted, over-emphasized, and promoted! It is branded as the "new normal," but on the contrary, it is just another ploy of our adversary to steal, kill and destroy what God so strategically created. Can the adversary really do this? With the consent of the created creature, that's the only way! Obedience to God breaks the vicious cycle.

So, is it the stability that we seek? You survey and be the judge! Man saves for retirement to create stability when his/her days of labor have ended. Man pursues what he calls "the American Dream," buying a home to provide a living space for his/her family. Everything we do is centered on creating this sense. But what we fail to realize is that it is only in God that our foundation becomes sure. It is in Him that life becomes predictable according to what has been written. Man can read the Word of God to discover the image of planned life. The outcome is sure.

See, God made this choice ours! The choice indeed is ours, but it can be devasting to our eternal fate if the wrong choice is utilized and implemented. So, God, in His infinite wisdom, already knew this part. It is man's responsibility to hear and obey. God had no secrets to hide from man right from the beginning. A lie was told to man that implied that God held out on man – not providing all that would make him equal to God. God never intended for us to be Him but to be like Him. Put this into perspective. We take things overboard – give man an inch, he takes a mile.

God gave us a sure word of destiny. In the beginning, there was an instruction that guaranteed His blessing, *"... be fruitful and multiply...replenish...have dominion... and subdue..."* (Genesis 1:28). How complicated is it to follow instructions to receive the best available? Apparently, very complicated! Daily we fail at the instructions that have transcended time. Generation after generation has come and gone, and yet, we still are creating our own self!

I remember someone that I know advised on social media to create yourself. I said, "oh, to create yourself is to imply that God didn't know what He was doing!" Why did I say that! The person went ballistic and blocked me from access to their profile – the whole nine yards! All because I stated the truth. They took it personally when it wasn't personal to me, but to them, it hit home, so I guess it was personal. Truth is personal.

Look at the instability that is in the land. God doesn't have any surprises per se! His Word is the road map that is a sure foundation. There is nothing to figure out, nothing to recalculate, no debates, no arguments, just His Word of blessing – to the obedient.

Man is known for his inability to be consistent, rather flighty. But God is not a man; so, in Him, there is no guesswork. He took the effort out of the equation and simplified it with the command. He said, do this, and this will happen. Do that, and that will happen. He left the complexities of choice to us. He did not opt to force or coerce us into any variations of His Law. He presented them in the package of His Dear Son: Jesus Christ. He wanted a larger family. Jesus's seed produced more for God's pleasure. Everything can be traced in His Word. We don't have to look far to understand these components; they are evident.

Trust what He does, what He says, He is sure! The stability that we seek is in Him. Ask yourself, what person walking on the earth has no variableness? Who is it that I can wholeheartedly trust without disappointment? Who is the first name that I call when something goes awry? Who is it that I share my deepest thoughts without breach? Who does not hold my past against me? There is no one living, but He Who is alive, Who came to eradicate the effects of my past – Him I can trust. Because with God, there is no guesswork.

SECTION II

EUCALYPTUS
Spiritual Fragrances

The Benefits of Eucalyptus?

In order to address "why," we must first address "what." What are the properties of Eucalyptus?

Eucalyptus is a multi-faceted herb that is used for multiple purposes. I see Eucalyptus as a healing-remedy agent. It has properties that reduce pain, just as God's word works in our hurt places, our weak places to build us up; it is our buffer that we need in order to continue. (Psalm 91:2)

Eucalyptus serves as a relaxation agent, just as His word when it comes in establishes, strengthens, and settles us by His grace. It causes us to have peace, not to fret or be anxious for nothing. The Word of God establishes the order in our lives when allowed to...

And this is how I am acquainted with Eucalyptus, by its medicinal properties to relieve cold symptoms, things that attack your immune system, just the same way there is a spiritual sickness that attacks our spiritual immunity. Its objective is to put us down, but when we begin to administer the medicine, we start to feel alright. Eucalyptus is the medicine for everyone.

And, what about being a breath freshener? Something for your mouth; to stop what comes out of your mouth from being distasteful and awful to those around you. It is personal sanitation. The word of God is to be spoken! What comes out of our mouths are critical! It can be sweet or cause someone to feel nausea by how bad it may be! The word of God spoken will be that breath of fresh air—the fragrance.

They say the Eucalyptus soothes skin irritations… skin irritants; what does that represent? It represents those things that have rubbed up against you. The things that we have ingested or come in contact with that we are "allergic" to, and we didn't know it! Just about anything can cause skin irritation. The word is like Benadryl—counteracting the reaction to those things that keep on rubbing you the wrong way. You know, like when our brother gets on our nerves because of how they are, the Word by His grace is the EpiPen for our anaphylactic irritations.

So, just like in the previous section that dealt with "needing an insecticide," Eucalyptus repels insects. Those critters in the spirit that lurk looking for space to rest, somehow or another, have found their way into lives through the cracks that we did not allow God the Constructor to seal! That's how Eucalyptus works; to rid us of.

It's a natural antioxidant that fights against certain cancers, heart disease, and dementia. The fragrance of God's word fights against those eternal life-threatening situations that spring up because of something we did not go to the doctor about. Sometimes, it just comes out of the blue, as far as we know! God's word, like Eucalyptus, is a natural and spiritual healing agent. His word deals with matters of our heart if we allow Him to do so… His Spirit fights against those dementia-like behaviors, situations, and circumstances that seem like it steals the memory of what God said about our circumstances. His Spirit brings it back to our remembrance.

Above all, the Eucalyptus tree can grow up to 50 feet tall. God's word is designed to tower over every other word that exists. The scripture says, if they speak not according to this word, there is NO light in them. This section is to identify those things that need healing; it is a perspective for you to recoup, peradventure you have forgotten.

Remember that God's word is good for those sensitivities in our lives, just like the Eucalyptus. "Take it and be blessed," saith Evangelist Valinda Wynn.

Get a Life! Stop Saying That!

Aren't we so quick to tell someone that seems boring to get a life? If they are a homebody, a tv watcher, not one that engages in the extracurricular, we say with emphasis, "get a life!" But do we know just what we are saying? Very little do we really know about those words.

Often, we blurt out words, phrases, and clichés loosely without the understanding of what is being said, like, "you are killing me!" Known as a figure of speech, but what are we really saying?

One would say, oh, what was meant is that you are making me laugh or making me feel some kind of way by what is being said (the euphemism). But we have no clue that we are really speaking some negativity over our lives - giving the devil in the atmosphere access to assault us, just how we declared it! Our words have life just as God's Word. Death and life are in the power of the tongue..." (Proverbs 23:7). If our words were insignificant, we would not need to watch what we say! There would be no scriptures reflecting idol words, of which we will give an account.

The bible declares that it is what comes from the heart that defiles a man, and what comes from out of him defiles him. (Mathew 15:18) We can't utter these words in gestures or figures of speech – are we speaking the truth or a lie? Speak truth to thy neighbor. (Ephesians 4:25) Provide things honest in the sight of men. (Romans 12:17) Why is this necessary? It is necessary to be as He is.

So "you are killing me; I going to give them a piece of my mind; you're hurting me; I love you to death" … all these euphemisms have life points attached, and one way or another, they will manifest. How then do you intend to have results?

Your Life Belongs to God

Why do you run as if you can get away from the purpose to which you were born? Why do you attempt to avoid the inner voice that continues to speak to you and through you? Why do you continue to operate or associate with meaningless nouns - pointing you in the wrong direction? What is going on? What are you thinking? Where is your mind? When will you learn? How will you overcome this? What will it take for you to accept the why of your existence? Please don't say I need to show you something else! Do you mean Words aren't enough?

Gee whiz, My protection doesn't do it? My everlasting Love - the mercy that I allow to renew every morning; MY unfailing compassion, that doesn't wet your whistle …? Hmmm! If I didn't know everything, your actions would stump ME. But behold, I am HE. The Supplier of eternity, the Giver of life, the Giver of Love and Salvation - I made it free. To you and to those that receive MY SON; the Way, Truth, and The Life, MY begotten One.

I knew you would not come right away, but at this juncture, it should be any day!

I protected you in your carelessness when you cared less about your own self; I was there. To pick up the pieces that you dropped or threw up in the air!

When you did not even consider the ones around you, I protected them from the onslaught of your actions toward family and friends.

You live so recklessly and aimlessly without. Walking in confusion, mystery, and doubt. Do you know why this is? It really shouldn't be. On too many occasions, I spoke directly to Thee.

I shared - gave you a glimpse of the greatness I planted on the inside. Every now and again, you stumble, and then you again backslide.

These steps backward trip you up. Gives you no protection from your adversary from a child to a grown-up.

I have always known your purpose beyond a shadow of doubt. Whenever you found yourself in a tight place, I'm the One Who got you out!

I centered you around people who showed you my love and my care, but as always, you wrestled and halted between two opinions, which led to despair.

I first asked what does it take, in essence, for you to come around? For you to be surrendered, prostrate – level to the ground.

You want this, and you want that, let ME tell you what I want. I'm going to be right frank with you; I'm not going to even front!

I want the investment that I made during the transaction. Your inception, your creation; I want your life.

Besides, it's mine anyway; I gave it to you before you were formed in your mother's womb. So, MY question is this, what are you waiting on, doom and gloom?

Can't you see you need ME to bring it all together? Your life is but a vapor and a very lite feather.

If you give ME yours, I will give you yours right back and give your life eternally. What's wrong with you because there's nothing wrong with ME!

Stop fretting about what happened or didn't take place. Put on your shoes; on your mark, set, go - run this race. It's not given to the swift or strong, but he that endures to the end.

This is nothing for you; you are used to "trauma… drama… baby mamas! "You were born for this, so - let's go!

Living In the Moment

What does that mean to you - to live in the moment? Life is not promised, but it is purposed with the time and destination of forever.

We often become preoccupied with the temporal when our lives are eternal— somewhere! So, where's it going to be: heaven or hell? Your ability to live in the moment distinctly depicts your eternal outcome.

Are you living to live again? You should be; because you will, but where? That is the question.

You might say, why do I need to live in the moment; why can't I just live? Have you ever noticed how time gets away from you, and you get caught up in whatever and still have not accomplished what you purposed? That's why! It's easy to get caught up in the wrong thing - caught in nothing.

Living in the moment constantly reminds you of purpose, taking your thought off what you see: the temporal. Rather, focusing on what you do not see - that's eternal, and therein lies your focal point.

Paying attention to the important, and not the flashing lights all around; that which appears to have so much significance; the bling of life; look away - it's a distraction.

It's a decoy to deter you from purpose. Get a grip! By now, you should know this!

So, you can't fix the past now, but you can maneuver from this point. Focus - put your glasses on; use the magnifying glass; do whatever is necessary to see beyond what is in front of you. The only way to live in the moment is to live in the moment. You decide to dismiss the temporary and cleave to the eternal! No one or nothing can preempt you from living in the right place - choose to do it! You can do it!

In a moment, in the twinkling of an eye… life changes. If it is that fast, you don't have time to daydream.

Released To Perform

We have a mandate, an unction to function. What is it?

We have an active declaration, released in the heavenly, that awaits our acceptance and permission, a purpose to which must be actualized to produce supernatural, God-given results! When is that?

No alternatives, delays, hits, or misses - just an ulterior motive that has been released to perform: Who did that?

It was designed with the wherewithal to bring it to pass; working knowledge to navigate results that please and profit - no holds barred; free to come forth and multiply: so, yield increase and bring forth that harvest! Where shall that be done?

Fruitfulness, multiplication, replenishing, dominance, subduing; the vitality to live for a specific purpose, time, and season: all granted! And when is this?

Yield, submit - submitting and yielding is the ONLY way to go, since you are clueless and do not know! In agreement to the word spoken, the Creative power to produce results for the purpose to which it was released: to perform.

The instinctive nature to obey the rule of the Finisher Who started and will perform as said. That's how it shall be done! That's the why? Now, what next?

Did not you hear me say what, who, when, where, how, and why? So, what's your question? Can you see the answer right in front of you? Grab it and let it activate in you. Allow it to manifest; the only one holding it back is you. It's already sent; package delivered; pick it up; take it to your house! Who leaves packages on the steps for someone to pick them up illegally? Isn't that why "the thief cometh not, but for to…?" (John 10:10). The thief sees your package was delivered; he is preying on you, not noticing that it has arrived!

Okay, so now you have it; it is inside your space. It was sent for intended use; let it go! Let it be free! Let it operate, takeoff, and produce. What's the hold-up now? You don't know how to…? Weren't you listening? I said, wherewithal was granted; instructions are engraved within; you need not ponder; its purpose is sure and known. Release it; its performance is guaranteed! Warrantied for a lifetime of sure productivity.

Stop holding on to it! Share, share, and share some more; there is an infinite supply of unction to function. Reservations-prohibited! Against such, there is no law. (Galatians 5:22) It requires you to do a thing: release it! Its active performance is based on you. I've already released it to you! Let ME do MY work in you, through you. The eye of your understanding is enlightened. You can do this: you have been Released to Perform.

Bravo!

Wanted but not wanted #got God

Do you know how it feels to be wanted but not wanted? To have a sense that your presence is a nuisance, a common disdain to the person who you care to be around? I wonder if God feels the same.

To say this just doesn't seem logical: wanted but not wanted. What in the world is this: truth! Let's look at the possibility of this phenomenon. Do you know how it feels to be wanted, but not wanted, thinking one way in your mind when other people despise your being, your existence, the essence of your person? You are like sandpaper to them, a scratchy surface that they choose to stay away from while your presence sharpens, smooths, fine-tunes who they are, but they only see one-dimensionally.

Do you know how it feels to be wanted, but not wanted, walking around life aimlessly without any person to celebrate your existence, to see you for who you are, and to accept your purpose? What is that like? God knows! (shaking my head) While you make them look good and they know it!

In my attempt to focus on how I was feeling at the moment, to be rejected by the person who I chose to be around, it was brought to me by the Spirit of God that this is the same position Jesus is in every time and every day we reject Him! If God were not God, I imagine that He would feel the emptiness of rejection, the loneliness of rejection, the worthlessness that rejection offers. So glad He isn't like us, who experience these types of feelings regardless of their validity and truth.

So why not be as God: needed, but not wanted! Don't you think He knows that we really don't desire Him as He desires to be desired? That the things we long for are not the things that pertain to Him at all? Our focus point: He is last on the list! How does He feel about that? How do you feel right now? He continues to provide!

So, get yourself together—comb your hair, brush your teeth, wash your face; it doesn't matter which order you do it in, just so that you do it! Move away from that wanted, but not wanted place; fill the void—all puns intended.

The Real Deal–Keep It 100

We must be certain that we are living in the space of keeping it real. Often, we shade the truth behind our desire because of our feelings toward a person or thing. On the contrary, shading is a lie!

Why am I writing this? Because I am constantly in a place of rejection or not being wanted in some sort of fashion. I have a close family member who does not bother, a family who can take it or leave it; seemingly, there is no significance to my presence. The picture is, I just exist! On the contrary, the thought of me merely existing is just a lie—I live!

Ok, if you live, then why is it necessary to go through this spiel? Didn't you hear me? I'm keeping it real—on 100! I'm saying it is being presented to me constantly as truth, but on the contrary, that picture is just a lie!

The other day, I was in an almost reckless experience with someone I love, who says they love me! The perception of what they said I said and displayed was so far removed from the truth; it was where they were; in this bad place, that they could not see the forest—skip the trees. They were blinded by their own thoughts, feelings, and projections, in such a way that everything

I said filtered from this negative place! Oh really, you mean to tell me that one could go someplace in their own mind and lose sight of reality? And the answer is, Yes. Animation can also sometimes be a lie, depending on what is being animated!

As I am writing this from a place of so-called rejection and withdrawal, I have a person in my life that is dear to me! Sometimes, I get these weird vibes that I am a nuisance to them and that they wish I just would not bother! Is it true? Yes, sometimes it is, but not always! There are times when I go somewhere in my own mind; then, my perception becomes skewed and overloaded with shade. We've already determined that shading is a lie.

During this writing, I come to understand that my perception of this is all wrong. Ok, what should be my vision? I'm glad I've asked! Jesus Christ and Him crucified! Looking unto Jesus, the Author, the Authority; the One, which means my starting point is in Him. The storyteller; the book Writer, the book of J… He wrote that; have you read it: probably not! Jesus is also the Finisher, meaning it stops with Him too. He is the conclusion of the matter, and since I am operating in His authority, my feelings have nothing in this! As a matter of fact, He is orchestrating this whole deal, by the way! He is the Author and Finisher of my faith, my belief, hope, goal, perspective, and what I look forward to and trust in! Period. He is my Expectation! So, what happens when we end up in this bad space? We've allowed our adversary and flesh to work game on us! We have the winning hand in the word of God; speak it—use it—know that it works!

Turn your thoughts forward. Release the past. As fast as it passes, it's as fast as we should release it… it's called living in the moment! Rejection is a feeling based on a specific thing, circumstance, or situation; It does not dictate one's life or value! Acceptance is the same; however, just as rejection, our dimension of it frames our existence and powers our attitudes as it engages our thoughts that become our behaviors. It's our choice—choose you this day!

Half-empty—half full, how are you seeing it? Don't lie to yourself; keep it real—on 100! Truth or not the truth; that is the question.

Gratefulness

Gratefulness does not bubble out of a closed mouth, a closed mind, a closed heart, or a closed soul. It comes from a merry heart, an open heart, mind, mouth, and soul.

Gratefulness is an attribute from God; for a man to give thanks for the things he has done... Give thanks for the things he (Man) has done, with the acknowledgment that it was of the Lord's doing, not his own ability and strength, that it was done. Therefore, WE ARE grateful.

Man has sense enough to say thank you when a gift is given; the desired gift; a small gift, a longed-for gift; a special gift from a special someone - a gift just because! We say thank you as many times as we feel necessary to let the other person know how grateful we are. Sometimes we even make a long-term obligation as an act or show of gratitude: not necessary, but we do it. But when it comes to the Almighty, it's short-lived.

We say thank You in gratitude for what we received at that moment and then become a selfish child that says what next? Ungratefulness is the antonym, the Nemesis of gratitude. How is it that we forget how good it is to be alive and to experience the beauties that living affords? The senses extend our ability to manifest the enjoyment of what we hear, taste, smell, and see. The chemistry that our natural flora maintains without our efforts. The mechanical nature of this body keeps going year after year.

Gratefulness is supposed to be as skin to us, something that covers us as a protective layer. Mends when necessary and repels when required. It has many shades of tones and many layers deep before it gets to the core of who we are.

Gratefulness embodies the essence of life's intention as originally mapped. It was the design of the Almighty when He said what was created was good! Nothing was intended as sorrowful, but we managed to change the course a little bit. God saw fit to send a body to reverse the curse, to remedy the breach in fellowship that separated man from his Partner – his Creator - his Life! It took God, in His awesome communion with Himself, to determine how He would brighten man's perspective again. He achieved His purpose!

We have been restored to gratefulness, a satisfactory record in Him. All that is needed is the receipt of it. No toil – no labor, not even delay; just open your heart and receive it with gratefulness. Return, O'man, to your original place!

What can I say?

Have you ever thought about how good it is to be alive? To experience the luxuries that living affords, that which money cannot buy.

Or is your focus more on what you don't have and how bad this or that is? What can I say - we were granted a luxury that death doesn't offer: time?

Time can be a great commodity that leaves room for many wonderful things to take place.

Time allows for healing, life, and for the dreadful: death.

Time: is the essence of what God created and gave as a gift to man. It wasn't rationed out; it was given in 24hours... one complete day. Did you know that one day with God was as a thousand years? What can I say, I can say, what am I doing with the time He has given me? Am I squandering it as if it were endless? Or am I maximizing its full potential; you know, the way God reviews it as much more than it appears. What does God see that we do not? He sees potential!

What can I say? It's Time to change our thought processes and mindset concerning life's perspective. See the beauty and essence that time has afforded. Live our life in the concept of a thousand years. One might say, how can I do that? Have you noticed that when you are doing something beneficial, progressive, or what you want to do, that time gets past you so easily, and you can get caught up for hours and not realize it? So it is when we walk in the purpose for which we were designed. Nothing is wasted - every second is maximized and appropriated for the good of mankind, just as the Creator designed. Nothing missing or lacking - broken, not! Only prosperity and provision because we chose to see from the broad perspective that the horizon allotted.

Look now, see the day and act like it is forever. For, after all, your real life is... Hmm, what can I say!

It Took the Love of God To Do It!

To love your enemies - You loved us when we were so-called not loveable: we were enemies of You. We weren't equipped with love—it was not what we knew.

You proved that loving your enemies was a prerequisite and something that could and must be done! You did it! You made us without excuse with our victory. You won.

When we were alienated - strangers of the commonwealth; we were made nigh by the Blood of Jesus. His death, burial, resurrection, and ascension made it possible, and through that blood, You freed us.

And now we are sons; and it doth not yet appear what we shall be; but when You appear in us, we know we shall be like You for all eternity.

Not only are we free to see You as You are, but to manifest Your person in our person to those near and those afar.

As we fix our eyes on You, You cause us to get to know You for ourselves; that this gospel might be preached to the world and be not just a book on the shelves.

So, let me switch this up a bit and forget about the rhyme. The objective of the Father is that He might gain your time.

We were walking in the flesh working those things which were not convenient, and such were some of you! But God, who was rich in mercy; wherewith He loved us, has separated us into a holy calling, engrafted us in, made us sit in, and has set us up upon a rock, and now - look at us! No goodness of our own; it took the love of God to do it!

It is Him coming inside of us and causing us to do what otherwise we could not: that is love. You interjected Yourself within and began to uproot that nasty sin. That cripples us from doing as we should. Obedience is possible and crucial for life! We can't love like we should until He is on the inside.

How could God ask us to love our enemies? Because He knew what it took to do so! He so loved that He gave... He gave up what was His - what was important. He sacrificed Himself to do it, all for the sake of love. Man is without excuse; God set the tone and has already given us the ability to do by His Spirit, where is your willing mind?

To will is present with me, but how to perform - I find not. That's what Paul said, but where is our excuse, our reasoning? There are times when "to will" is nowhere to be found; what's the excuse then? It is at that time that we have the I don't want to's?! It's like a disease; it is a spirit that works against the purpose and order of God. If it is not with Him, then it is against Him. We make excuses for our flesh to continue therein. It took the love of God to do it, bringing us into the knowledge of the truth.

Understand that without God is without the ability to do anything. For without God, we can do nothing. All things come through Christ's strengthening power, not of ourselves. God insisted on us experiencing His love toward us and favored us so! There was no sin too great to override His love that was for us! It was not possible. But God wherewith He loved us hath quickened us; He made us alive. It was a jolt in the spirit, a tug at our person that this is something new and to pay attention to; duplication is.

When we did things to others that we knew were no good and could cause them a problem later. God in His wisdom, forgave us when we repented and blotted out our mess! He made it possible! Make no mistake about it- "He took the possibility of the impossible out of the impossible so that it would be impossible for the impossible to be possible." (Emphasized) Just as strange as it sounds, it is as real as what He did: it's radical belief! If God says to do something, rest assured; you can - if you want to.

If God did it - made us in His likeness and His image; we can do it too! It will take the Love of God to do it! So, do you love Him? If so, then keep His commandments! You can do this!

Overshadowed To Change The DNA

What on earth does this mean? Overshadowed to change the DNA—who's DNA—mine? How is this humanly possible; well, it's not! It's an inward deviation of an unformulated calculation with an outward quantitative and quantified manifestation that alters DNA.

Ok – And what about this overshadowing? What about it?

How does this happen?

Just as in the day of Mary prior to giving birth to the Savior. The Angel of the Lord paid her a visit to bring glad tidings of great joy. Great joy: to be ridiculed, talked about, and possibly on that day, stoned to death. What joy can come out of that? The joy of the Savior's birth that started the path for you and me to be whole and reign with the Father after man's sinful nature squashed the plans of God seemingly, temporarily. This same Jesus did the same thing as His mother; He gave up Himself for the means of others. And Hebrews tells us, "…Who for the joy that was set before Him endured the cross, despising the shame, and is set down at the right hand of the throne of God." He had to die, He came to die, and He did. His death to self - took place for the overshadowing to manifest. Because He did, look at the result. We can talk about Him, live for Him, and be like Him in every way just because we allow Him to change our DNA.

Like Mary, His Spirit overshadows us and impregnates us with that holy thing. The thing we are incapable of possessing or giving birth to except we say, "...be it unto me according to Thy Word" and let it be so! Luke 1:38

What God intends to do is change the effects and override our natural history; only God can do such a thing. It's all we know, but to God, it is insufficient. We must be adopted by the Beloved as a son. In doing so, there is no compromise or concession to operate in the past!

Who, what, when, where, and how doesn't matter here; only why you are here is relevant at this point! You don't have a choice to retrieve the work of the past; you can't go back and get who you think you are/were; it's under the blood: literally.

The scripture hath said, "Now are we sons of God, and it doth not yet appear what we shall be..." (I John 3:2) You mean to tell me; this thing is still evolving? Do you mean there is more from where this came from? Oh wow, this is an overwhelming truth! He gave us the power to become sons of God. (John 1:12). What power is needed here? The inward deviation of an unformulated calculation with an outward quantitative and quantified manifestation that alters DNA. Oh, now I see! Wasn't that easy?

Natural parents are carriers and become insignificant going forward once you have responded to the call of God on your life. It's between you and God now. Do this! It's all about sonship – God's child for life. This overshadowing is necessary to become… there is no other way!

Look, I took the time to get you here; I took you beyond your years - you stopped! Jumpstart and live like a king!

My Way

Things, people, and places can't always go my way. Sometimes I try so hard to get things, people, and places to maneuver to the beat of my drum; it does not always go my way.

In my frustration, I have a tantrum of some sort; even if it's internal and no one ever sees it, it happens! My adrenaline rushes, my heart beats, my pulse pulsates like a blender with a smoothie mixture in it - it's germinating; it's breaking down; it's chopping up because I didn't have it my way.

Why is my way so important? Is my way the best way? Is my way the only way? Do I think that my way is the right way? All those answers are displayed in my behavior when it does not go my way.

I am reminded that there are two scriptures, not just one, but two scriptures, that say there is a way that seems right unto man, but the end thereof, are the ways of death. (Proverbs 14:12 and 16:25) It was so vital; it was spoken twice. We try to interject our way in everything, even with God; it doesn't work like that.

You are not controlling this; this will not allow you. There is your way, my Way, and the right way, which is considered best practice? Whichever is - do that!

Time - the Appropriator's choice

How is time determined - By one's perspectives, one's objectives, or one's plan? On the contrary, it is God's time, not ours.

The Creator is He; producing and manufacturing as He so chooses - everything that exists came from the essence of the Creator's life-giving ability breathed into man's purpose (for/of) becoming.

What happens when the manufactured is no longer used for the essence to which it was designed? A house unused loses its habitability, the functionality to provide adequate existence for one's coexistence. It begins to deteriorate from the inside out! Why? Because the essence of its purpose has not been appropriated. Every stretch of the imagination of dilapidation, erosion, and break-down manifests; how so and why, because life stopped! As the inside erodes, shortly afterward, it is noticed by every visual eye that life isn't there. Shingles fall from the roof, dirt and debris collect, and the weeds - they grow wildly! The show of breakage from the house to the sidewalk—evidence of no life—becomes a hazard to those around it!

What about a car? The same essence is true. A car left on the street, unattended, abandoned, and unused, also loses its essence. The dormant, unbothered, not operated, unattended vehicle evidentially loses air in its tires for no apparent reason; the air hadn't been extracted; it just oozed out! Why? The life of appropriation stopped. Thieves, predators, and violators consider this unmarked car a target of continual destruction, vandalism, and demise at the hand of man. They take the true essence of functionality away, "strip it, and leave it to be an eye-sore" for its viewers without regard for its potential. After a while, its purpose is headed for the landfill/junk pile, the graveyard for vehicles, to end the furtherance of potential use. And what about the house? Internal deterioration that leads to external manifestation loses its curb appeal until it is deemed condemned; nothing and no one is safe in or around it; it is eventually "torn down" - replaced with something else.

Time and the essence of NO life did this! The house didn't choose - neither did the car, but what was it that caused the disdain of abandonment; the search for something better, an out-grown taste considered no more? The inability to produce and/or function in its full intended potential - who can say except the inhabitants and/or the owner. They decide the time span of its existence. The car and house don't realize that its inability to provide habitation and/or transportation to the liking of its attendee will cause life to cease as it was once known. Consider medicine. After a period of "time," it too loses its potency, lifespan, intended capability and ability to function and produce to its maximum potential. It then must be discarded - no longer safe to ingest! Hmm!

What is being said here is; time is not ours but is determined by our ability to continue to provide the essence of life, functionality, adding to its existence. However, it is extended by use of care and maintenance by its Appropriator; no extensions are granted for non-use. There is a limited warranty, a manufacturer's clause on its lifespan, and an expiration date. Regardless, it will expire without the appropriation of life.

Time is determined by the Appropriator - the choice is 'not' yours!

What Day Is It?

Well, Well, Well!
Of all the days in the world
It happens to be a specific day,
A special day, the perfect day to celebrate
Not just anyone, but you!

You make me laugh
You make me smile
You make me cry for a while
When I think about just how special you are to me!

There is no one that I'd rather celebrate than You!
No one I'd rather honor than
My love, my soul mate, come true.

Being with you brightens my day!
So, I'm happy to say; come what may.
We've been blessed in every way
Besides, it's our Birthday
Oh, Happy – Happy Day to you, and me too!
Because we are ONE.

To my Love, Cliff
J

There's No Such a Thing

Why do we say that? How can we feel like that? Had we not considered ourselves: our raggedness? The mercy that was shown. The mercies of God—His grace when it was not merited! There is no way we deserved it, but it was granted! Huh, there is no such thing!

We hear this so frequently, so carelessly stated, so misunderstood and yet! We have the audacity to place others in that category - wow, such gall! You know what; there is no such a thing!

When I consider who I was, am, and going to be, I can honestly say that God so…, and therefore, there is no such a thing. The expectation has been set and already established in the heavenly, we cannot deviate from the example. As a matter of fact, your enemies get it too; God covered everything and everybody - no one is exempt, so again, there is no such a thing.

Jesus gave His very life to show this truth on the earth: there is no such a thing! If it were so, you would not be either. Love is not an option but a mandate for characteristics: it is your ID. There is no such a thing as the unlovable. If that were true, then no one would love you!

Consider that!

Are you Offended?

The good that I do is to the glory of God.

So, what, if there is no acknowledgement; never any! What does that mean to you? The fact that you are awakened to it means that you have the potential to be "a glory stealer:" a thief.

Why do they have to call your name when you give? Why does the word about the alms you do and give need to publish your fame to glory? Why do you do what you do? To be seen of men or to be seen of Me!

Aren't I the target of your attention? The One you've chosen to please. That pride you have is telling Me you need to spend more time on your knees.

I placed you here to bless Me, to do good as I empowered you. To do as you recall to your mind, more than has been done to you.

That attribute of selfishness didn't come from Me to you. You picked up that spirit when you allow pride and jealousy to come live in you too.

After all, I gave you purpose, one with free will and choice. To ever lift up the praises of Me, with a resounding and continuous voice.

So, why that sad countenance when they deliberately ignore your works. If it's Me you seek to please, know that their disdain for you will only become worse.

I don't think you get it; the path is a repeat. The one I chose for you, My Son walked, it ends in no defeat.

Relax and let it go; this offense is only to hinder. If you really knew and longed to be with Me, My thoughts within you would engender.

My everlasting love and new life I give freely; so that you would have ample opportunity and space to be with Me eternally.

Over and over, I keep telling you; it is to My glory. Loose him - let him go; and walk in My liberty.

Unfortunately, disobedience is the option that I never meant for you to have. It yields death, Hell, and the strength of My wrath.

Have you got it yet - is it in your spirit, written on the tables of your heart? Offense is not a one-time thing; it is a practiced and mastered art.

You say, the good that I would, I do it all to the glory of God. All In truth, all in righteousness, not pretense, and not in Fraud.

If that is the case, then why are you offended? Erase it! Put a smile on your face. Pick up your cross and run My race.

It is not given to the swift nor strong but to the one that endures to the end. The same shall be saved; the same is he to whom one does not offend.

Now, are you still offended? Come, Follow Me!

SECTION III
LAVENDER
Spiritual Fragrances

The Reason for Lavender

What qualities does Lavender possess? It has properties for bathing, relaxation, cooking, and as a perfume. It can be used topically as it diminishes the appearance of skin imperfections. It reduces stress and is also good as an aromatic due to its calming effect. What is being said here?

Lavender as a Spiritual Fragrance is like a neutralizer to anxiety and its components. When we are feeling overwhelmed, Lavender uses its properties to overcome those effects that cause us to move away from God into our flesh.

Lavender is an eye-opener, a vast reality of the truth. Its potent abilities can often be an irritant to the skin, and it needs to be coupled with a carrier oil to reduce its sensitivity. What am I saying? The Word of God is Lavender, which needs to be coupled with love for sensitivity's sake. The scripture says, "The Word of God is sharper than any two-edged sword..." It pierces, divides asunder – dissects; its depth goes to the core of man - bone, joints, marrow, soul, and spirit! (Hebrews 4;12). There is nothing hidden; everything in its path shall be affected. This is only one aspect of these various possibilities.

Spiritual Fragrances

This section of Lavender is just an in-your-face type of deal! It deals with matters of the heart, covering all grounds. There is nothing shaded, scaled back, or diluted. "Take it and be blessed." *(Evangelist Valinda Wynn)*

"Heaven has Chosen Me; So, You Don't Have To!"

Here is your aromatic, inhale it and go on and live.

So, doesn't that sound a bit cocky? Of course, that is not the intent to sound special, but the truth is what it is: truth!

Favor of God has nothing to do with me or you; it's His purpose to prosper me! God sees to it that I have what I need. He ensures that I am protected, even when I am careless with my own! His mercy is prevailing to keep me from falling and present me faultless - faultless; what kind of party is this? It is God's party, and He gave me a personal invitation. All I need to bring is me!

God's strength is made perfect in weakness. Weakness that is made perfect in Him. God designed this so that we don't need perfection because He makes all things perfect and new! God is doing this, and it is marvelous in my eyes.

The choice is preference. Choice can seem callous and may feel impartial - leaving no room for opinions. Heaven has chosen, so you don't have to!

Concessions, accolades, or kudos are prohibited - it's all God. There is no repayment plan; a yielded life will suffice because of His yielded death! Realizing that opinion judges' merit, God threw it out; who am I to remember - and who are you?

Can't handle the prosperity, oh well, take it up with God; it's His choice!

Wow, it seems so arrogant! No, not really, just sure that heaven has chosen me, so you don't have to!

Heaven's signature is not temporal but eternal; it cannot be reversed. Why try! Think about this etching in the stone. You should adopt this prehistoric truth!

Time and Purpose

Time coincides with purpose. The problem with time is that it has a limit that purpose cannot exceed, violate, or extend. When time is up, the purpose is over.

Purpose is subservient to time; it is not reversed. One should never dismiss time because of purpose. On the contrary, you should consider time because of purpose.

Time allows you the space to carry out your purpose; without it, nothing will be produced. God made everything in six days-it was the window of time that He created to establish His purpose.

Don't you see, the two go together? They are like Frick and frack, Night and Day, up and down, and breakfasts' bacon and eggs. When you hear of the one, you know the other is nearby. They are one spectrum to the another, but they are together, at least to who is considering.

What is being said? Time is progressive, and so is purpose. If time is continuously moving in its purpose, how come you are not?

Get busy! Purpose won't wait – there's no time.

"Keep thy heart with all diligence; For out of it are the issues of life." Proverbs 4:21 (KJV)

"Thy Word hath I hid in my heart, That I might not sin against Thee." Psalm 119:11 (KJV)

"For where your treasure is, there will your heart be also." Luke 12:34 (KJV)

Caught

Don't get caught in the fast life - at the moment that snuffs life.

Don't get caught repeating the same thing over and over and over again -
when you knew it was time to get off the wheel.

Don't get caught in the hype of what you see!
Don't even get caught up chasing money!

Don't get caught up in chasing people.
Don't even get caught up with chasing yourself!

I simply say, don't get caught. But I will say this,
Catch up to the Word, and let the Word catch you!

"And Jesus said unto him, No man, having put his hand to the plough, and looking back, is fit for the kingdom of God." Luke 9:62 (KJV)

"I press toward the mark for the prize of the high calling of God in Christ Jesus." Philippians 3:14 (KJV)

Just do it!

Just do it
What do you have to lose!
Rather, what you have to gain should be the question to ponder.

You've spent so much time wasted in why not!
Why not bask in why you should, because I said so!
Just do it!

This is not only an expression that Nike adopted; this word was here before them, before him. I mandated this execution; don't you feel it; sense it in your spirit? All lights are go! You need not wait...
Just do it!

Trust your heart and do it. Trust those thoughts and do it! Ride on the momentum of inspiration. Launch out into the deep, catch the fish, and reap the harvest - it was and is intended for you to profit.

Do you really need Me to push you? I already have! I've given you the perspective to go and just do it!

"I call heaven and earth to record this day against you, that I have set before you life and death, blessing and cursing: therefore choose life, that both thou and thy seed may live:" Deuteronomy 30:19 (KJV)

"And if it seem evil unto you to serve the LORD, choose you this day whom ye will serve..." Joshua 24:15 (KJV)

"No man can serve two masters: for either he will that the one, and love the other; or else he will hold to the one, and despise the other. Ye cannot serve God and mammon." Matthew 6:24 (KJV)

Choices

Many of us, all of us, have them. They come with the territory! There's no manual per se that walks us through each scenario of life. Well, not one that we know of initially, and the one that we gain ready access to, most times we reject. So, what are these choices?

God gives us a time to…! He gives us "free will," the ability to pick what we want. It's the fruit stand of life. If the bag of apples that we got had one and a half apples that were rotten, would we throw the entire bag in the trash, or would we get rid of the problem? Most just discard as needed. Some will use the good parts of the rotten apples. Ewe… what! Use the rotten - yes, the rotten. Keep the good and throw away the bad! If that's all we had to eat, it would not be a question; we'd do just that! So why then do we handle life as if we had nine lives, not that they really have them either (cats)?

Where am I going with this? We get one bag of apples. Now, we do have the option to pick out the bag. We can see what we want, but sometimes we are blindsided by what appears to be ripe, just to find out that there was rotten in the bag with the purpose to soil them all! What, all the apples we have? Please, talk sense to me! What are we talking about? I'm talking about our life—that's the bag and those apples—different aspects of our lives. Some Macintosh, some Honey Crisp, some Fuji, some Gala (these represent the various cultures, lifestyles, and purposes). Those real sour Granny Smiths, those make the best kind of pies and tarts - they're sour, though! We always want the sweet, the fruit, the pleasant - the sugáre! Don't judge the apple by its initial flavor – give it some time!

See, the baker understands the apples' potential and the level of knowledge, skill, and ability required to exact the greatness of those different kinds of apples. So, we leave it up to the expert to show us what to do with this variety!

Do you hear me? Let the BAKER, who is GOD, decide what to do with the apples! We've got this in the bag with one life to live!

"19. And out of the ground the LORD God formed every beast of the field, and every fowl of the air; and brought them unto Adam to see what he would call them: and whatsoever Adam called every living creature, that was the name thereof. 20 And Adam gave names to all cattle, and to the fowl of the air, and to every beast of the field…" Genesis 2:19-20 (KJV)

"For as he thinketh in his heart, so is he…" Proverbs 23:7 (KJV)

"Death and life are in the power of the tongue; and they that love it shall eat the fruit thereof." Proverbs 18:21 (KJV)

"For Verily I say unto you, that whosoever shall say unto this mountain, Be thou removed, and be thou cast into the sea; and shall not doubt in his heart, but shall believe that those things which he saith shall come to pass; he shall have whatsoever he saith." Mark 11:23 (KJV)

DECIDE

Time changed in the garden. Man lived as God - walked with God in the cool of the day; so, what happened? Man decided to do something other than his purpose to walk with God; to be that friend of God! Was there something greater than a friend of God? I can't see it! But in some way, it was acted out rather arrogantly. Man was like Lucifer - he had his own agenda!

God gave us the same thing that He has: choice. He gave us choosing power. You decide! Whatever you call it, it is!

He gave us speaking power. Whatever you say, it is. He gave us thinking power—as he thinks in his heart—so is he. You cause yourself to be as you are! Didn't you know this? Think about it!

Can't you do better O' homeless one? Come home and live. You are not despondent; everything you need to thrive has been given to you at the beginning of time! It's in you - you can make it; activate your God-given tools! Thrive—live; live—thrive; do both! You've got this!

What starts in your mind can be executed to the doing of the thing. You decided to be outdoors; decide you're better! The Creator is in you: create and be like unto Him.

Just remember, don't let time repeat itself. You can never take God's place - don't try! Your fate is sealed: don't mess it up! Your identity is already established!

Don't let pride dictate your destiny. Don't let your "eyesore" govern your response; focus on purpose. See life as it was meant to be seen. Everything is NOT about you! You can move from the place where you are when you decide.

Get right ready! Your decision is required!

Stupidity: Who is to Blame?

What is stupidity - it is the behavior that shows a lack of good sense or judgement. Consider this: which one did you operate in; lack of good sense or judgement? Where do the chips fall with you? Are you willing to accept the fault finder, or are you still passing the buck?

Did Uncle Charlie do it because he touched your breast when you really didn't have any? Was it your sister's husbands that introduced you to something that never happened? Who was it? Why are you in this clouded place, acting like a scarred animal? You are the superior, the one that was given the authority to reign, dominate, subdue, and replenish! So, what are you replenishing? More anger about what didn't happen?

You didn't die when you were given that stuff that could have "killed you!" Can't you see your life can't be taken by man - so stop acting like it can. That woman you married - that dogged you out; left you and went to some other man, and now, she is pregnant by him! You gave her the best that you had: your name, and she declined it! So what!!! That's her loss! Move on - she wasn't it! The plot of your adversary failed; you are still thriving, wounded but thriving.

So, what was it for you; good sense of judgement you were lacking? No disrespect given! This is not a slap in the face nor a negation of circumstances. It was true, it did happen, but it didn't accomplish its purpose for most! Why, for most, because they chose from which perspective, they'd function... tell me, is it the lack of good sense or judgement.

You call it out yourself; don't leave the nameless writer to determine what it is for you. Break the cycle - stop letting people control your actions - don't be a puppet all your life! Move away from insanity; you know the meaning, the one that we blurt out when talking about others while we excuse our lack.

Come on - can't you see what has happened? Actions based on nothing! Rejection - yup, you were, but by who? Someone who couldn't see pass their past. They were operating in the world: don't judge their poor sense of judgement; let them come to it! You come to it and stop blaming others and accept where you are!

Howbeit you have given away your authority, your decision-making power? If I were talking about someone else, you would call it Stupidity! But since I'm talking to you, what do you call it?

Speaking My Heart

S peaking my heart is not always the easiest thing to do, for a number of reasons. Sometimes one is not safe to speak freely without misunderstanding, misreading, misleading, and/or misinterpreting. One's echo from the heart should be crystal and not mud.

One might say, when I speak from my heart, it is not received in the manner in which it was intended. Was it not what was intended? It's hard to speak contrary to what one really feels about a person, place, or thing!

Why is it that periodically, expressions manifest that seem condescending or from a place of rejection? It may be that the root is contrary to what is tolerated, projected, or displayed. Because He made us spirit; the spirit does know.

Why does one become persistent in rejection or denial? I don't know, but the laws of nature provide this fact to be truth... rejection causes gravitation, which makes no sense at all.

So, why is it necessary to write this today? I already said I was speaking my heart.

The End

"The heart is deceitful above all things, and desperately wicked; who could know it?" Jeremiah 17:9 (KJV)

"For sin shall not have dominion over you..." Romans 6:14 (KJV)

"...but the tongue can no man tame; it is an unruly evil, full of deadly poison." James 3:8 (KJV)

Gray Hairs

I was riding in my car going to breakfast one morning with my husband. When I gently pulled down the mirrored visor to observe my presence, hair, face, etc., you know how we women do it! I suddenly noticed an excessive number of gray hairs, and boy, were they unruly.

They were peeking up from under my natural wavy pattern; they made themselves front and center on the nape of my head - all around my hairline; for all to see! There was "no shame in their game" - they had it their way! No matter how smooth the edging of my hair was, the more they seemed out of place. It took nothing to stand out in the crowd, not looking apart! Those gray hairs!

Now, my normal routine with my hair is brushing it back in a bun of some sort, as I slick it down with some kind of gel; then, I tie it with a satin cap to lock in the wave pattern until the style is solidified. All of this, I did that morning before leaving home - I promise you! But some way or another, you couldn't tell that I took any time to groom those unruly gray hairs. It was as if they had a mind of their own, their own agenda, a rebellion of some sort. It made me chuckle to think about gray hairs and the ones that normally manifest these gray hairs.

Now, I mean no disrespect of any sort; there is great wisdom in many of our colorful-haired men and women; however, I often find this similar attribute present in more than just hairs! Why is it that when one has seniority in any area, there is nothing no one can tell them? "I've lived long enough to know a thing or two!" Well, isn't that the same with any person? Why does age bring about the entitlement of superiority, knowledge, privilege, and right? Sometimes our gray-haired loved ones become belligerent and combustible for no apparent reason. Why? The same reason why those gray hairs would not lay down, no matter how much gel, brushing, or tying up was done - they would not comply... period!

Have you ever met anyone who behaves like those hairs? They are hard to get along with, hard to manage, hard to tame; as a matter of fact, there is no taming at any point. It's their way or the highway! No reasoning: and they know everything about everything, and everybody! Those persons are just like those gray hairs. They are in-between the transition and refuse to give in! If you haven't met anyone like that before, look in the mirror, like I did, and introduce yourself! LOL

The Birth of a Flower

Who can find a flower that evolves whole: none! A flower has a process in which it develops and manifests its rare beauty and essence. It first starts with a seed, and then the germination process begins. Human life is the same.

The day comes; just a seed, no life, no structure, not even purpose, until God hand-picks, just as we pick any flower that we see. But this is a different pick. There was no beauty to behold of it, only in the Master's eyes. It seemed to have no worth, just a zygote - evolving from chromosomes that would eventually become an embryo.

This flower started before anyone could see it, small and insignificant – looking as if there were no hope. But the Master called forth life and spoke into its existence - giving it a time to evolve into purpose. He assigned a caretaker to provide the much-needed nurturing and watering - making sure that weeds didn't kill it along the way. The caretaker was hand-selected, regardless of their imperfections: God chose. Why them; because He was/is the Master Landscaper Who ensures that the flower comes to full circle and purpose.

After the care is received, whether adequate or not, the fullness of time begins to break through the ground and show its real character. The beauty of the flower that remains in the care of the Landscaper yields provision. Their job is to prune and nurture as it blooms for all to see! Its life span all depends on the caretaker's ability to care for it, and so are you in the hands of the Master Landscaper!

You are the flower that God carefully picked. You are the flower that was assigned to experience everything that you've experienced. He knew that your kind of flower could "...*endure hardness...*" Your type of flower can *bloom wherever planted*. Your sort of flower "*takes a licking and doesn't stop ticking.*" You are the flower that takes some time to break through; overcome the weeds and attacks to annihilate life; regardless, you do come forth!

Consider the beauty of your character – the essence of your life – the promise of your purpose; you have everything to live for because the Master Landscaper said so… and it is so! Why look ye at the process, in which you've evolved, that doesn't matter now; the Everlasting Caretaker Who ever lives to make intercession for you took the assignment of your care. You only have one choice: bloom, oh ye flower – bloom!

Behold your beauty; the essence of your Caretaker is in you. Designed to live as long as the care continues, so live and show the world what manner of flower you are. You broke through already; "…it is finished." Make use of your finest hour. Enjoy your day, life, and destiny in the Master's care.

Forever and ever.

So it is; your birth has come!

To you, "Jeremiah," as you are called, you know who you are.

Unchangeable

Who determines a sister? Not you - not DNA, your mother, or your father; only God.

Who determines a friend; not you - not people, not even experiences, but the Bible declares there is a friend that sticks closer than a brother, and His name is Jesus? (Proverbs 18:24)

Who determines a confidant, a counselor—one who has a timely word that can bruise and soothe all at the same time? Not you - not even a shrink or a preacher!

Who determines the time spent, the distance between, the love that is endless, regardless of time and space? Some things just can't be changed! Breath, character, and integrity are consistent components in any sphere of life - They are the nuclei that link us!

Who is who? That who is you! Designed to be…, destined for purpose, and linked for greatness. Sisters for life! Some things just can't be changed; they are embedded truths - here now and forever.

Forever Loved - For a minimum of 70 years!

For You Yvonnla S. Graves

Who Am I?

I am not who you say
I am not who you think...
I'm more than that.
My identity has been hidden.
Can you find Me?
Nope, you've got Me all pegged wrong!

Who am I?
Not your average person who lives from day to day.
I am a King and a Priest.
Yet, you treat Me like a peasant.

You ignore My daily contributions
My extravagant essence.
My ability to get the job done.
My being there on a whim, without much effort

My being able to keep your secrets, cry with you,
laugh with you, share with you.
Yet you treat Me so insignificantly. Why?
Haven't I shown you who I AM?
Your Shoulder to cry on - your Friend.

Do you mean to tell Me; you are still not sure of My being a part of your life?
Wow, that tears me up!

All those times, you should have failed.
I was right there to assist you in that project.
I had your back and your front; don't you remember?
Oh, I forgot; your memory is short when you are the one in need!

You used to call me Friend-now you don't call Me!
You used to love My presence; now you consider Me worthless.
Who AM I to you? I can't tell!
That doesn't change Me. No matter what you do, say, or think, I will always be.

I Am!

The Pastor's Wife - My Dear Sister

This writing is for you. I have observed your behavior, person, and attitude, and I have somewhat to say to you.

As you know, I am a writer. I can just sit down and begin to write on a whim. This writing is not easy to write, but hopefully an easy read with a win-win!

It's Subtitle: BE SURE.

I have been reflecting on many things since coming to your vicinity.
Knowing that my purpose was not melodious only, but prayer was the number one key.

I began my task some time ago in the hope that we would come to know.
The expectation of God in full effect.
I am waiting for His manifestation yet.

I would like to share with you the sentiments of my heart, of which I believe it is the heart of God while utilizing my art.

Spiritual Fragrances

On a few occasions, there have been some deviations – some missteps, to be exact.
Please let me share my observations and carefully share them with tact.

Your place in the house is critical, as one would say.
The wife, the lady, the member - those positions ranked every day.

Many things have been observed as your character attribute.
Your ability is openly seen and is seen as one astute.

Your poise and posture are sometimes very sharing.
At times those same things may be perceived as OVERBEARING.

Why overbearing if ones' heart is in the right place?
Because it is who is observing that determines the values face.

Positions are as such to generate lanes in which one may travel.
But when those places become skewed and jumbled, things begin to unravel.

The Elder, the Reverend Doctor, or his government name, is in fact, the husband, the pastor, and a member too.
But to the people, he is the man whom God has chosen to use.
Ok, and what does that mean to you and me?

It means so very much!
Enough that a writing has been crafted,
that you might gain a sense of such!

It is imperative that the manservant remains sanctified in the eyes of the congregation.
WE have a responsibility to maintain that creed and to do it without defamation.

It's been a few times where a contradiction has been publicly displayed.
In the behavior of the people, these same actions - rest assured will be replayed.

How then can one chastise - the people be corrected?
If that which is to him has not been redirected.

The wife, the lady, the member, the first partaker of this essence.
The torch carrier, the head honcho, is the director of the progression.

You choose the pace to which the people follow.
The temperament, the attitude toward whether full or whether hollow.

Why do I care about what you say and do?
Because I share in the heart of God, and I too love you.

You are a great asset to the kingdom and to your vicinity.

What you set in motion now will be set in motion for eternity.

Because I believe your heart toward God, and you mean the best for this house.
I am certain you will make an honest adjustment while assisting and honoring your spouse.

This is not a "pin your ears" back writing; it is to illuminate with the light; of what we the people can see, and not for you to walk as one in the night.

One might say it's my perspective, and I would say that's true!
But we must BE SURE that we cause no stumbling in anything We Say and anything WE Do!

BE SURE!
I'm Just saying…

Stationary Movement

The Oxymoron

Who wants to be used by God?
Are you willing to travel?
Are you ready to go?
Are you flexible to the stationary and the nomadic?
Will you allow God to move you from one place to another while standing still?
Are you willing to let Him do that work on you?
As you do, God will work in you to will and the to do of His good pleasure.

You must be positioned in Him, in stillness - in the quietness of your spirit, while He flows you through this life as living waters with a strong current.

You Must BE STILL MOVING.

Life Has Meaning

"For in Him we live, and move, and have our being…" (Acts 17:28 KJV)

During my normal routine of grooming myself, I was at the nail shop on this particular evening getting a pedicure, my routine procedure; but there was something a bit different about this time.

Prior to my 5 o'clock appointment, I had to go to the bathroom, so I went home. After my due diligence, I headed to get my phone jack to plug up my iPhone while the nail technician worked on my feet, but this time I heard, "why not talk today." So, I decided to obey what I heard and leave the charger at home. I got in my SUV and headed to the nail shop.

When I arrived, I parked my car; I noticed a black car with a woman that was in all black. She was an older woman who parked her car in the middle of the street as if she didn't know what she was doing. She stood out to me, but not enough to stop what I was doing. I went in and sat down in the seat as I would normally do

- endeavoring to make the selection of what color I would use this time. As I sat, here comes that same woman; she sat two seats over from me. Her nail technician was an Asian gentleman who apparently spoke little English. She said, "I'm new around here… This is my first time here!" She repeated this several times. It came to me to welcome her. So, I said, "Ma'am, I heard you say you were new around here; Welcome!" That lady lit up like Christmas! She said, "oh, thank you…!" The conversation began.

This no-named woman at the time began to sing my praises for being a good person - she didn't know me! Here is this black woman talking to this older white woman in a predominantly white nail shop in a gated community. Do you see the scenario? But because life has meaning, where you are does not matter; it's Who's you are that makes the difference.

As we talked the entire time that we sat in those chairs, she said, "I love you already." Of course, I blushed! Just earlier today, I wrote about being wanted, but not wanted - feelings of rejection that flooded my soul. But because I heard what God said about talking… and I obeyed, something wonderful happened this evening. Not because she sang my praises, but because I heard God and obeyed and lit up this woman's heart with the love of God.

As we were talking - getting close to finishing time, it came to me again to take care of her tip. So very awkwardly, it took her a minute to get money out; I, too, did not have cash and had to download Venmo for my technician and did the same for hers. She almost didn't know what to say, let alone thank me, as one would normally do. I paid, we left, and that was that!

Ok, then what is the essence of this story: know your place and purpose? Discern what your assignment is and only do that! Remember, life does have meaning – don't take it out of context!

My Debut

What is a debut? It is a first appearance or performance in a particular capacity or role, the first public appearance of a new product or presentation. So, when does this take place—do I decide? Well, I'm glad you asked; to a certain degree, you do, but not so much!

Your entrance when you were BORN announced to the world your arrival, your distinction, but not your purpose. Your parents had no inclination of the exactness of your debut, but only the possibilities. Your purpose remained a mystery to you and those who made your acquaintance. You couldn't be planned for real; parents are not the givers of life; it was the breath of the Almighty that did this! (Job 33:4) So, what is this life that made a stunning entrance into the world with a purpose unknown? It remains to be seen. When do you arrive?

So, you've made your first appearance into the world in one capacity; are there any others? God knows. Is it to arrive and then to die? God knows. Is it this unclear distinction that is anonymous to the world, including you? God knows. You say, Listen, I know He knows, but when will I know? I'm glad you asked; When He makes His debut in you.

SECTION IV
CYPRESS
Spiritual Fragrances

When Is CYPRESS Used?

Of all the oils around us, what is the significance of this Cypress? Let me give you the backdrop of how I came to use the name.

When I reconsidered the names of these four sections of Spiritual Fragrances, the name Cypress just came to me. I heard it before because I am an avid user of essential oils, but never did I use or examine its benefits; I just said, this section shall be named Cypress. The mystery unfolded when I looked up Cypress and its contents.

Cypress is a unique tree that you can often find in a Cemetery. They are associated with death mainly, but there are some other properties as essential oils that can be quite beneficial.

Cypress is also commonly used in spas for massages, relaxation, etc. It is said that it has a "grounding effect," which makes it beneficial to use in the time of transition or loss. So, Cypress is an atmosphere changer. It helps one cope with whatever disparity they are facing. It can bring one to a place of hope and peace, a functional place, just as God's word of encouragement does for us – it brings us to a place where we can go on! Encouraging words have that kind of effect on humanity.

This is a very small section, but it has been an encouragement to those in whom it has been written. Be blessed by it.

Only Remember

Although, losing a loved one is quite a difficult experience. I hope that as each day progresses, you will remember the memories shared and use them as steppingstones to bask in the joy of having them in your life for that pre-destined time.

Mourning is necessary; remembering the joys of life is better. Be lifted in your spirit; cherish and relish the memory of your beloved!

Peace and Comfort to you and yours!
For You K. Navarro

"We are confident, I say, and willing rather to be absent from the body, and to be present with the Lord." II Corinthians 5:8 (KJV)

"And as it is appointed unto men once to die, but after this the judgment:" Hebrews 9:27 (KJV)

"Jesus said unto her, I am the resurrection, and the life: he that believeth in me, though he were dead, yet shall he live:" John 11:25 (KJV)

I've Got This

Now, you can move. You can do as you should.
No reserve, no apprehension, just instincts that obey My rule.
Here, I've designed freedom, liberty, tranquility - the place of rest, peace, and praise, removed from labor, hustle, bustle, and toil. No man-made devices are in place, just My rule.
You have the liberty to come and go. Without delay, without dismay - every day - it's ok; you are good now!
Time is of no essence. No decay, no breakdowns, My rule forever in place to guide you, lead you, govern you, pick you up, and take you. It's My discretion.
Your life - the runway, the ramp for takeoff; one way or the other, a flight is necessary to get to your next destination. I AM the pilot in this aircraft; all you need to do is yield and fly.
No fight - just flight; My rule in place lifted you - now REST.
For you, Dad – Reverend Dr. Deother Melvin - RWG

What a Time!

What a time, what a time, what a time!

Who could govern such a time; a time to love, a time to live, a time to cry, and a time to die! It's a part of the package deal with fringe benefits.

Who could govern such a time, to receive the rest of the Lord, to bask in the beauty of His splendor, to celebrate eternity - holy, holy, holy, is the Lord God Almighty? No pain, no gain required - eternal reward, paid in full!

The trouble I've seen, I'll see no more! Eternity is forever cherished - with no need to further explore. It's a done deal at this point; the ease of living has just begun. That victory is now celebrated in His ambience; I've won.

As for you who remain to cherish my memory, don't let it be a blink in time. Remember, life is but a vapor, a thin and passing line. From there to here – newborn to senior, it is your life's choice to make. So choose it wisely and be deliberate, for it is your fate that is a stake!

Cry no more! You can Rest in Peace, too, living life in Christ and letting Him be seen in all you say and do. There is a time to do whatever, but this life is not it! For one day, you will come to the end of your journey - your time to call it quit.

As for me, resting in the word of Jesus, I am now at peace. In hopes that you will live to celebrate your forever life as you embrace your release!

And what a time this is!

For your Uncle Deacon Jeremiah Melvin - RWG

REFERENCES:

(The Hebrew-Greek Key Study Bible 1984) (Spiros Zodhiates 1984)

Eric Zielinski DC (Dr. Z), "Gold, Frankincense & Myrrh – The Truth about

Their Significance," Natural Living Family, 6 January 2022

https://naturallivingfamily.com/gold-frankincense-and-myrrh/

Britannica, T. Editors of Encyclopedia. "How Deadly Is Quicksand?." Encyclopedia Britannica, Invalid Date. https://www.britannica.com/story/how-deadly-is-quicksand.

Merriam-Webster.com Dictionary, s.v. "the American dream," accessed February 8, 2022, https://www.merriam-webster.com/dictionary/the%20American%20dream.

John Heywood's 1546 Collection of Proverbs

The Holy Bible King James Version Copyright 2002 Thomas Nelson

Scientific American. "Odds Favor Drunk Trauma Victims." Scientific American. Scientific American, October 1, 2009. https://www.scientificamerican.com/podcast/episode/odds-favor-drunk-trauma-victims-09-10-01/.

www.doTERRA.com Essential Oils

Cover Designer - Fiverr: akramdesigner1

Editor – Fiverr: Arialinawrites

Logo Name – Fiverr: Marrygigvilla

Shutterstock Royalty Free Images

Image: 1305237625 – cover crown

Image: 1841797672 – cover clouds

Image: 751128052 – cover perfumes

Image: 275157605 - Cypress

Image: 788845840 - Lavender

Image: 56466718 – Frankincense & Myrrh

Image: 1906938967 - Eucalyptus

CPSIA information can be obtained
at www.ICGtesting.com
Printed in the USA
BVHW031529240722
642887BV00010B/860